THE RED AIR FORCE AT WAR

BARBAROSSA AND THE RETREAT TO MOSCOW

Recollections of Fighter Pilots on the Eastern Front

THE RED AIR FORCE AT WAR

BARBAROSSA AND THE RETREAT TO MOSCOW

Recollections of Fighter Pilots on the Eastern Front

ARTEM DRABKIN

With contributions by
Mikhail Bykov (research and aircraft profiles)
Alexei Pekarsh (introduction)
Andrei Sukhrukov (appended interview with N.G. Golodnikov)

Translator
Bair Irincheev

English text
Christopher Summerville

Pen & Sword
MILITARY

First published in Great Britain in 2007 by
Pen & Sword Military
an imprint of
Pen & Sword Books Ltd
47 Church Street
Barnsley
South Yorkshire
S70 2AS

ISBN 978-1-84415-563-7

A CIP catalogue record for this book is
available from the British Library.

Typeset in 11/13pt Sabon by
Concept, Huddersfield, West Yorkshire

Printed and bound in England by
Biddles Ltd

Pen & Sword Books Ltd incorporates the imprints of Pen & Sword
Aviation, Pen & Sword Maritime, Pen & Sword Military, Wharncliffe
Local History, Pen & Sword Select, Pen & Sword Military Classics
and Leo Cooper.

For a complete list of Pen & Sword titles please contact
PEN & SWORD BOOKS LIMITED
47 Church Street, Barnsley, South Yorkshire, S70 2AS, England
E-mail: enquiries@pen-and-sword.co.uk
Website: www.pen-and-sword.co.uk

Contents

A time will come, a fearsome time, when the enemy will walk over this land, and all the land will be entangled with barbed wire and iron birds will be flying in the sky hurting people with their iron beaks. That will be already before the end of this world ...

A. Kuznetsov, *Babi Yar*

List of Plates

Introduction

As soon as a human being invents something he will apply it to the destruction of fellow human beings. The most outstanding invention of the early twentieth century – the airplane – was no exception. Soon after the birth of flying machines came the prestigious trade of Air Force pilot. And within that privileged caste – inhabitants of heaven – fighter pilots formed an elite: for they were the only ones tasked with aerial combat, and as such, became gladiators of the skies.

The fierce dogfights of the First World War and the record-breaking long-distance flights and races of the 1920s and 1930s captured the imagination, causing boys across the world to become obsessed with flying. As youngsters they built models of planes, and as teenagers attended glider schools and flying clubs. Upon graduation the best students became Air Force pilots. In the Soviet Union the popularity of pilots like Gromov, Chkalov, Kokkinaki, and those airmen who took part in the 1934 mission to rescue the crew of the ship *Chelyuskin*, crushed by ice in the Bering Strait, can only be compared to that of film stars. In a country where many people had never seen a steam engine, any profession related to machines was prestigious, and a person who could handle an airplane was especially respected. A smart uniform only increased this sense of awe. For at a time when boys walked barefoot during summer – in order to save their only pair of shoes for winter – and adults wore simple clothes of linen and shoes of canvas, pilots sported long leather boots and a dark-blue uniform of fine woollen fabric. Emblazoned with their distinctive insignia, they certainly stood out from the crowd. And like tankmen, pilots often wore medals and decorations awarded by the State – a rarity at that time. Finally, pilots were well paid and had all their needs met by the State. That said, the training of pilots was initially the preserve of flying clubs, which in the early to mid-1930s only existed thanks to membership fees paid by individuals or voluntary *Osoaviakhim* societies. Club members underwent training in their spare time, while holding down regular jobs.

But in the late 1930s came the slogan: 'Our country needs 150,000 pilots!' It was only then that flying clubs received State grants, instructors obtaining wages comparable to those of Red Army commanders. Club members were now required to study full time, moving into dormitories where uniforms and food were provided. Many younger students were obliged to quit school in order to complete pilot training. As well as volunteers for whom flying was a lifelong dream, many random people entered the flying clubs for pilot training. This was the result of a deliberate campaign to enrol as many *Komsomol* and Communist Party members in the Air Force as possible. Some of these recruits simply did not have a talent for flying; others, however, became excellent pilots. In this respect, the Soviet Air Force was unique: no other country recruited pilots on a draft basis.

After sitting exams at a flying club, superintended by Air Force instructors, graduates were sent to their next training stage: an Air Force academy. If in the early 1930s this training stage lasted about 2½ years, by spring 1941 it had been reduced to a minimum, due to the sharp increase in pilot numbers. Flying schools with four-month training courses were formed (implying that cadets had completed basic flight training in flying clubs), while Air Force academy courses lasted ten months. But aerobatics were forbidden and this had an immediate impact on the graduates' level of professionalism. Training was confined to simple take off and landing procedures, other elements being considered secondary. As a consequence, fighter regiments received young replacements with only eight to ten hours of flying – and often in a different type of plane to that used by the regiment. Such pilots could merely hold the control stick, having no understanding of aerobatics, dogfighting or foul weather flying. And these would-be fighters had a limited amount of fire range training, for most graduates of the flying schools and academies only received two or three sessions of fire practice at a canvas cone towed behind a plane. As a result, they did not know how to use gun sights correctly.

But it would be wrong to state that all Soviet fighter pilots had this background. By the summer of 1941 the Soviet Air Force included pilots with a high level of training from the mid-1930s, their skills honed by battle experience gained in Spain (1936–39), Khalkhin Gol (1939) and the Winter War with Finland (1939–40). But their numbers were insignificant compared to the burgeoning crop of new flyers.

But a bitter blow befell cadets graduating between 1940 and 1943: this was Order No. 0362, announced by 'the pilot's best friend', People's Commissar of Defence Timoshenko. The order declared that graduates were no longer to enter the Air Force as lieutenants but as sergeants. Furthermore, graduates were consigned to live in barracks – supplied, paid and equipped as NCOs – until they notched up four years' service. Barred from sporting the pilot officer's badge they'd dreamt of since childhood (worn on the left sleeve, it depicted a propeller, wings and crossed sabres in gold, on a blue background, surmounted by a red star, and known colloquially as a 'Chicken'), many took offence, expressing their displeasure by refusing to wear NCO rank insignia. Timoshenko's Order No. 0362 not only caused bitterness among graduates, it also broke the military principle of subordination, as technicians and ground crew – often lieutenants – were obliged to make their maintenance reports to pilots classed as sergeants.

* * *

In contrast with the Red Army Air Force, the German Luftwaffe of 1941 consisted of carefully selected volunteer pilots. And by the time a young German pilot arrived at his unit he'd already accumulated 250 hours' flying practice, including aerobatics, group flying, foul weather flying and so on. German pilots were also trained to handle any situation – such as emergency landings – while dogfighting (in groups or as individuals) and ground assault were emphasized. Upon arrival at the front, German pilots were not sent into battle immediately but placed in reserve groups, where their skills were improved by instructors with battle experience. Only then were Luftwaffe pilots deemed fit to fly combat missions. In 1941 the German system of training was one of the best in the world.

And with regard to tactics, the Luftwaffe was superior to the Soviet Air Force. Luftwaffe tactics were developed after thorough analysis of combat experience gained in the Spanish Civil War. The cornerstone of the German system was the deployment of fighters in free formation of pairs and fours – the mainstay of fighter aviation during the entire Second World War. This system gave German pilots great flexibility of manoeuvre. It also allowed them to maximize their advantage in speed. The Luftwaffe also had radios, something the Soviet fighter pilots of 1941 lacked. Thus the Germans enjoyed both tactical and technical superiority at the outset of the war.

In addition, the Luftwaffe cultivated independence and initiative in Air Force commanders at all levels, a German fighter pilot being free to fathom the best method of completing his mission. Soviet pilots could only envy their opponents in this matter: before a sortie they would be given not only the area of operations, but also the speed and altitude at which they were to fly. Under such conditions Soviet pilots could not react to quickly changing circumstances. One must also remember that during the early part of the war flyers were often attached to ground armies, whose staff officers frequently displayed a vague notion of Air Force tactics. For example, pilots were repeatedly tasked with long patrols at low altitude and low speed, 'So that our infantry may see our Air Force in the sky all the time and feel confidence'. Naturally in such circumstances, Soviet planes were easy targets for high-speed German hunters and suffered heavy casualties as a result.

* * *

Without doubt a big factor in the Luftwaffe's superiority in the first years of the war was the vast experience of its pilots and generals, gained during two years' heavy fighting, predominantly against the British Royal Air Force. The USSR, on the other hand, largely ignored the lessons of earlier conflicts. But as time passed the situation changed. For a start, the Soviet training system was drastically improved. The air schools and academies continued to provide minimal training but pilots would no longer go into battle straight from class. Instead, graduates were sent to reserve air regiments to receive additional training on the types of aircraft they would be flying in combat. The large numerical superiority of the Soviet Air Force facilitated this change in training, which permitted 'green' pilots to become familiar with combat flying gradually.

Technology also improved, more new Soviet fighters receiving radios, permitting pilots to be guided and controlled from both ground and air. It also meant that fighter pairs could operate at longer distances from each other, in loose formations and at different altitudes. As a result tactics improved and group commanders became more flexible in their command decisions. Meanwhile, combat experience and the behaviour of the enemy was actively studied and analyzed. All these factors influenced the course of war in the air, although the Luftwaffe remained a strong opponent till the end, capable of delivering heavy blows and fighting bravely: but it could no longer win the war.

*   *   *

The prevailing notion expressed in countless history books is that Soviet victory in the air was achieved by simple numerical superiority. Hopefully this book will help the reader understand the true nature of that victory, for it gives a voice to the main witnesses of the struggle: the pilots themselves. Here for the first time Soviet fighter pilots – ordinary flyers, not celebrated 'aces' or commanders – are given a hearing.

It is well known that aerial fighter tactics do not give pilots even conditions for scoring 'kills' or 'victories'. And not all fighter pilots had a chance to show their skills, especially those assigned to Air Defence or escort duty for ground assault aircraft: the former encountering enemy fighters infrequently and the latter being primarily concerned with deterring enemy interceptors rather than seeking them out. Indeed, statistics show that over 80 per cent of fighter pilots did not score a single 'kill'. These were the wingmen, whose job involved covering their leader – the real 'scoring' player. Thus, while lead pilots had a greater chance of notching up victories – winning decorations and promotions in the process – wingmen had a greater chance of being shot down. But the real story of air combat over Russia belongs to the latter group: rank and file flyers that bore the brunt of the war. It is through their eyes that this book focuses on the fight in Soviet skies.

When reading the accounts contained in this book, aficionados may question the authenticity of some episodes, especially with regard to numbers of 'kills' claimed by Soviet pilots. Suffice to say that discovering the real number of 'victories' scored by a fighter pilot is a rather difficult problem! For a start, it is important to distinguish between a 'confirmed kill' and a damaged enemy plane. In theory, a 'confirmed kill' referred to the destruction of an enemy aircraft as approved by a strict set of rules – a system observed by all air forces of the period. But in practice it was usually enough for a pilot to claim a 'kill' with the backing of his comrades or ground observers. But the very nature of a dogfight – including sharp changes in speed and altitude – frustrated objective reporting. And the statements of ground observers (even those describing events seen directly overhead) were often useless, as it was seldom clear who had shot down whom. These problems were aggravated by the sheer numbers involved in the large-scale air battles over Stalingrad, Kuban and Kursk, where hundreds of planes fought from dawn to dusk. It is therefore likely that many 'kills' claimed by pilots actually made it back to their airfields. On average, the ratio between claimed and actual 'kills' – for all air forces of the Second World War – was between 3:1 and 5:1. As for monster air battles like the ones referred to above, the ratio was more like 10:1.

Meanwhile, other factors have contributed to the confusion surrounding the issue of Soviet 'kills'. For example, in some cases comrades passed on their victories to colleagues, in order to help them win a decoration. And in other cases commanders claimed subordinates' victories as their own – the so-called 'prerogative of the superior'. Finally, the Soviet practice of recording shared victories as well as individual victories in pilots' logs obscured the picture even further.

The idea of awarding decorations for group or 'shared' victories came about as a morale-boosting exercise in the early days of the war, when successful engagements were rare. Inexperienced pilots, flying into combat without the benefit of radio communication, were thus rewarded for 'kills' scored by their unit as a whole. Later, as the Soviet Air Force improved its technological and combat performance, the emphasis switched from collective merit to individual merit, pilots receiving honours primarily for individual victories. But as a large pool of pilots already had many shared victories to their name, some regiments simply recounted them as individual victories, thus ensuring their men were rewarded. For example, a pilot with five individual victories and 25 shared victories might suddenly find himself with 15 individual victories and five shared victories. Thus a pilot could be turned into a fighter ace and 'Hero of the Soviet Union' overnight. Indeed some staffs of large units – armies for example – didn't even bother to recalculate a pilot's tally: any individual victories required for a decoration were simply picked up from his unit's shared victories.

Of course, after several decades the difference between confirmed/ unconfirmed and shared/individual victories can be vague in the minds of veterans. Meanwhile, the archived lists of pilot victories, which are supposed to clarify the matter, are often incomplete. Frequently they don't even match the number of victories recorded in pilots' flying logs, decoration citations or other documents. This may be explained by a shortage of archived reports concerning specific periods. For instance, documents relating to the early war period, from 1941–43, are particularly fragmentary.

As for the veterans themselves – although they naturally remember their dogfights – most prefer to relate stories of comrades or daily life at the front rather than personal achievements. And this is what makes their reminiscences so precious, for they offer an insider's view of a world that is becoming more remote with each passing year: the world of the wartime fighter pilot. The archived documents that remain – written in 'officialese' and often plagued by mistakes and exaggerations – are no substitute for the immediacy of real battle experience, as told by the survivors of that victorious generation. Some of the veterans whose memories are published here passed away while the book was in the process of editing. We hope the present work will help you, the reader, understand what the war meant for them; how they managed to hold out and win.

This book contains interviews with Russian fighter pilots and ground crew, collected during the period 2000–2006 in Moscow and Stavropol. Having gathered more than 20 interviews with fighter pilots, the material was divided into two distinct groups: those who took the first blows of the Luftwaffe in 1941 and those who came after (the latter group serving under the skilful command of the former). The present volume contains interviews with veterans who began their service during the first six months of Operation *Barbarossa*. They experienced the defeats of 1941, the painful rebirth of 1942–43, and the ultimate victory of 1945. During this odyssey they matured from 'green' pilots into experienced flyers. Survivors of innumerable dogfights, these warriors provided the leadership for a new generation of pilots who came into service later in the war.

Artem Drabkin and Alexei Pekarsh 2006

OPERATION BARBAROSSA

CHAPTER ONE

Vitaly I. Klimenko

As Told To Artem Drabkin

I first met Vitaly Klimenko at a Moscow veterans committee. Surprisingly energetic for his 82 years, he arranged the interview in a straightforward, business-like manner. I visited Vitaly in his flat and spent several hours discussing not only military service but also his post-war experiences, when he was sentenced to five years imprisonment for 'anti-Soviet propaganda'.

Why did I become a pilot? That was the fashion of our time! Pilots were heroes: Chkalov, Levanevski, Lyapidevski, Kamanin, Vodopianov, Gromov. We wanted to be like them. I was born and lived in the Zamostie region of Sudzha, a town near Kursk. Older guys from our town would go to study at the Air Force academies. They would come back on leave in beautiful uniforms, in leather coats – you see? So I decided that only the Air Force would do for me! I was dreaming of getting a leather coat, a smart uniform, and of flying a fighter plane. With these dreams – and with the recommendation of the *Komsomol* – I entered the Rogan Academy for Pilots and Navigators.

Upon arrival we rookies were sent for a steam bath and then split into companies – later they were renamed 'flying squadrons'. We began our service with basic infantry training. The first week we spent in barracks, each recruit receiving a bed and bedside table. An infantry sergeant major ordered us to fall in, then marched us to the barracks of the 1st Company. The first thing they taught us was how to make our beds properly.

A week later we pitched tents on the airfield. We spent the whole summer and autumn in camp, studying Red Army manuals. Training stressed firing drill for both the Mosin rifle and the Maxim machine gun. We also played soccer, basketball, volleyball, light athletics and did some boxing. We had sports competitions, hiking, orienteering all the time. I remember we would get so tired we could not wait for 'taps' to sound. But a few months later we got used to the routine. We completed basic training in winter, passed our exams, and were sworn in at the banner of the academy in spring. Only after this were we officially enrolled as cadets.

In the spring of 1938 the Rogan Academy for Pilots and Navigators was divided into the Rogan Navigator School for Flight Observers [i.e. navigators – Ed.] and the Chuguevo Military Air School for Fighter Pilots. I was worried they might make me study the navigator's course, but luckily I was enrolled in the fighter academy. Back in Rogan we'd already begun studying flight theory, navigation, Morse code, topography, physics, mathematics, medicine – as well as aircraft hardware. But before we started our flight training we were subjected to medical and loyalty inspections. Some cadets, whose parents had been deported as *Kulaks* or arrested on charges of a political nature, were immediately dismissed from the academy. At Chuguevo we were split into squads of 10–12 cadets. My squad leader was Pavel Kulik, a pal from the Donetzk Basin, a keen and diligent worker. The bed next to mine was occupied by Eugene Zherdij.[1]

It was as late as April–May 1938 that we were split into flights of seven or eight cadets, each flight receiving a pilot instructor, and we began studying the U-2 aircraft. My flight was led by Lieutenant Mikhail M. Karashtin. At the same time regulations loosened and we were permitted to take leave, visiting Chuguevo and Kharkov. The first thing we did in town was take pictures and send them home to our parents and friends.

In October 1938 I received a month's leave and went to visit my parents and younger brother Nikolai. I was still a cadet and not allowed to wear the 'Chicken' insignia on my sleeve, but as a rule all cadets ordered tailor-made uniforms to their taste, which were beautiful. I did the same and returned home in a mixture of cadet and officer uniforms. On the left sleeve of my tunic and overcoat was a 'Chicken' insignia, my *Budyonovka* was of officer style, and I had a wide officer's belt with a big star on the brass buckle – all of which were strictly forbidden in the academy. Besides this I got my leave pay. It was a lot of money in those days and one could have a good life! Back home I would go to the only restaurant in town, and to cinemas and dances. My old friends were very interested in planes and flying. I told them honestly that I had been in the academy for a year and as yet there had been no flights!

So the time for my first flight came. Lieutenant Karashtin,[2] my instructor, was in the front cockpit and I was in rear. My pilot's helmet was connected by a hollow rubber pipe to the instructor's helmet – that's how we communicated. An order to start the engine came. A technician stood in front of the plane and some cadets would put 'sleeves' on the propeller tips, connected to thick rubber bands about 15m long. The ends of the rubber bands were pulled by the cadets until the 'sleeves' finally slipped off, causing the propeller to rotate: at that moment I had to turn the handle of the magneto to start the M-11 engine. This was repeated several times until I found the right moment to rotate the magneto so the engine would start. Much later we stopped using rubber bands and began pulling propellers by hand in order to start the engine. Once the engine started the instructor told me to warm it up. There were no brakes on the airplane – it was held back by two bars on the ground, which blocked the forward movement of the wheels. When the engine was heated sufficiently – running on low throttle – the instructor ordered the bars removed. The next order was to taxi the plane for take off. I taxied to the starting line and lifted my hand, asking for permission to take off. If the runway was free the inspector would wave his flag. I remember the instructor warning us not to grip the joystick too much – some cadets clutched it so tightly the instructor had a hard time taking off and landing!

Finally we took off and flew 'around the box' – the four sides of the airfield – at an altitude of 100–150m. The instructor asked me: 'Do you see a tractor over there?' – 'Where? I don't see it.' – 'What? Are you blind?' I looked closer. Indeed there was a tractor on the ground: 'I see it!' – 'Good job,' he replied; 'Now we are landing.' Later he told me: 'You don't notice objects well, you should work on it.' I was gutted: 'God forbid they dismiss me!' But nothing happened. I flew about twenty times with an instructor instead of the usual thirty. Mikhail Mikhailovich told me: 'Vitaly, I want to try letting you fly alone.' I replied: 'Maybe I could fly with you a bit more?' – 'No, you are doing everything right.'

What is the most important thing in a first solo flight? The main thing is to level your plane about 1.5m from the ground during landing. Sometimes you would see a cadet levelling his plane at a height of 10m. The instructor would shout to him from the landing mark: 'Hey, you'll need a staircase from there!' Thank God I had no problems with this, while some cadets were dismissed from the academy because they couldn't estimate altitude.

Then we began studying aerobatics. At first it was hard to loop-the-loop: if for some reason you got stuck upside down, all the dirt and dust from the cockpit floor would fall on you! We continued the U-2 training programme in the winter of 1938–39, using skis for landing gear. As well as aerobatics we began studying flying in threes: it was not easy to keep the correct distance between the planes. We were also trained to fly in formation and to navigate according to predetermined flight paths. Thus during 1938 we had learned take off, landing and aerobatics: including deep bends, combat turns and spins.

In spring 1939 we switched to the UT-2. That was a faster and more demanding plane. I didn't wreck any planes but other cadets did: some even crashed. When a plane crashed the whole squadron would be grounded until they repaired the plane themselves, under the guidance of technicians. When we completed training on the UT-2 we shifted to the I-16 – a modern fighter but very demanding, especially during take off and landing. First we learnt to manoeuvre on the ground, on old planes with wing surfaces removed so we couldn't take off by accident. A cadet would get into such a plane, start the engine, and give it almost full throttle. He would roar across the airfield, imitating take off. It was important to gain speed, lift the tail, and hold the fighter on the runway. It was a complicated exercise and some guys failed. There were cases when someone would not manage to keep the plane on the runway and it would turn sharply, breaking the chassis. When this happened training would stop until the plane was repaired. Of course everyone would be upset that training was suspended – especially the one who had wrecked the plane! These ground exercises lasted between six and eight weeks, after which we started flight training on the I-16.

I graduated from the academy in September 1940, having studied four types of aircraft and with a total flight time of 40–45 hours. After completing the academy course we were commissioned as lieutenants. Only then did they issue us with Air Force uniforms – something I'd been dreaming of since childhood! They did not give us leather coats, however, saying we'd receive new ones when we joined our units: but this never happened, which upset me very much!

I was transferred to the town of Shaulai, in the Lithuanian Soviet Socialist Republic, where I joined the 10th Fighter Regiment. Upon arrival we six graduates of the Chuguevo Academy were distributed between flying squadrons. We were billeted in private apartments in Shaulai and officially employed as fighter pilots with a salary of 850 *roubles* a month. We were also attached to the regimental canteen, located in the garrison. We would have breakfast and lunch there but dine in the garrison canteen. They only paid a quarter of our salary in *lits*, which was quite enough for living: the rest was sent in *roubles* to the border customs bank and we'd get the money on the way home. While there was a shortage of goods in Russia – everything was rationed and people led a poor life – Lithuania's shops abounded with food and consumer goods. In one shop I found a pair of beautiful foreign-looking shoes, but it turned out they were made in Russia at the 'Paris Commune' factory: but you could never get shoes like that in Russia! I also bought myself a Swiss Longines watch. All these belongings were left in my apartment and lost during the retreat.

As already mentioned, we lived in private apartments. I lived with the family of a Lithuanian Army officer, who continued his service in the Red Army. His infantry unit was based in Vilno [i.e. Vilnius – Ed.] so he only visited his family at weekends or when on leave. Meanwhile, another pilot of our regiment, Junior Lieutenant Viktor Volkov, rented a separate room in the same apartment. The Lithuanians treated us well – we would even dine together at weekends and during holidays. We paid for the apartment through our support unit, the so-called Airfield Service Battalion, which was stationed next to the airfield.

Our regiment had three squadrons: two had I-16 fighters and one had I-15s. I was sent to the 1st Squadron and a plane was reserved for me. I already thought of myself as a fighter pilot, but when experienced pilots checked our flying skills they said: 'Guys, you still have much to learn!' And so we studied the I-16 practically from scratch. Meanwhile the flight commander would reconnoitre the area around the airfield in a UTI-4 before giving the go-ahead for independent flights 'around the box'. Flights were not made on a daily basis, as the airfield was a small grass meadow capable of accommodating just one squadron at a time, so while one squadron flew the other two made repairs or had theory classes. And we had to share the airfield with the 46th Bomber Regiment, which used the facility a couple of days a week for training.

On Saturdays we usually attended officer classes. We studied German planes and the new MiG-1 fighter. At the end of these classes all our notes were collected by the NKVD special department, as the MiG-1 was considered a top secret plane. But the main thing was flight training. We practised aerobatics, dogfights, and firing drill: shooting at cones towed by another aircraft or at ground targets.

The border with Germany was near – just 100–125km from Shaulai – and we could sense its proximity. First, the Baltic Special Military District carried out military exercises round the clock. Second, our airfield always had one squadron – or at least one flight – at full readiness. We met a lot of German spy planes in the air but we had no orders to shoot them down, so we simply escorted them to the border. Why did they scramble us to intercept them? To greet them or what?! The answer is not clear. I remember we also patrolled at low altitude over Shaulai during the elections for the Supreme Councils in Lithuania, Estonia and Latvia. I don't know the reason for this – it was either a holiday show or intimidation.

Of course we had our private lives, too. We made friends and would go to the Shaulai garrison's House of Culture, where we would sing, dance or watch movies. We were all young – just 20 years old. I had a beautiful Lithuanian girlfriend named Valeria Bunita. I met her on Saturday 21 June 1941 and we agreed to go to Lake Rikevoz next day ...

At that time we were at summer camp, sleeping in tents as the exercises of the Baltic Military District were in full swing. I awoke about five in the morning, in order to have time for breakfast before picking up Valeria. But I heard planes buzzing. The I-15 fighters from the 3rd Squadron were on duty that morning – we dubbed these planes 'coffins' as there were accidents with them all the time – so I thought it was a dummy air raid from Panevezhis and those 3rd Squadron guys had missed it. I flipped my tent open and saw planes with German crosses firing their machine guns at our rows of tents: 'Guys, the war has started!' – 'Fuck you, what war?' – 'See for yourself, it's a German air raid!' We jumped out of the tent – some of our neighbours had already been killed and wounded. I pulled on my flight overall, took my map case, and ran towards the hangar. I ordered a technician: 'Roll out my plane!' The 3rd Squadron's duty planes, lined up on the field, were already burning. I started the engine, jumped in the cockpit, and took off. I circled the airfield as I didn't know where to go or what to do! Another I-16 fighter approached. He dipped his wingtips, indicating: 'Attention! Follow me!' I recognized Alex Bokach, commander of the sister flight. So we flew to the border. We saw burning villages and columns of advancing German troops. Alex dived and I saw smoky bursts spitting from his plane as he strafed the column. I followed suit. We assaulted those columns and it was impossible to miss: so dense was the mass of enemy troops on the highways. For some reason they didn't return fire, their AA guns remaining silent. I was scared of losing my leader – I didn't know my way back! We made two passes then returned to the airfield and parked our fighters in the hangar.

A car drove up from the regimental CP: 'Was it you flying?' – 'Yes it was us.' – 'Now let's go to the CP.' So we drove there. The Regimental Commander said: 'Arrest them. No flights for these two. Who permitted you to strafe those columns? Do *you* know what's going on? I don't. Maybe you are responsible for an act of provocation. Maybe those were friendly troops . . .' I thought: 'Damn it! They'll demote me to hell and I'll lose my two rank cubes. I've just been home on leave as a lieutenant and all the girls were mine – how can I return as a private? I don't want to go home as a private!' But when Molotov made his speech at noon we were transformed from hooligans into heroes. We were the only ones from the entire regiment who fought back at the Fritzes without waiting for orders. But our losses were high – many planes and hangars were destroyed.

I remember one of our squadron commanders flew the only MiG-1 on the afternoon of 22 June – he alone had got to study this machine. We spotted a German reconnaissance plane and the Squadron Commander approached it from the rear but didn't fire. I thought: 'What the hell are you doing?!' The MiG returned to attack the Fritz again but still didn't fire! When the Squadron Commander landed we walked up and asked what was wrong. He replied: 'The trigger didn't work.' But the trigger was only covered by a security frame – he just had to flip it aside!

By the end of the day we had 12 undamaged planes on the air-field, which experienced pilots flew to Mitava Airfield at Riga. The personnel of the regiment retreated on trucks and refuelling tankers – any vehicle that could move. We retreated with the infantry, artillery and tank crews. We had fire fights with small German groups and some bandits. At first we only had pistols, but little by little we got more weapons from infantrymen – a machine gun and hand grenades. In Elgava they welcomed us with machine-gun fire from a first-floor window. We approached the house and threw several grenades through the window. The machine gun shut up and we drove on.

At Riga Airfield we met our comrades and I got to fly a scouting mission. Next day we were supposed to escort our bombers, tasked with raiding the advancing Germans. They were supposed to fly to our airfield and pick us up: but instead a German bomber force flew in from the sea and gave us a proper pasting. We hid in trenches. All of a sudden someone fell into the trench and something started dripping on us. The air raid over, we scrambled out and beheld our comrade: he'd been in the latrine when the air raid started; the air pressure from the exploding bombs had thrown shit all over him! Dead and wounded were all around but we couldn't help laughing.

There were between five and seven fighters left in the regiment, which we handed over to other units. Meanwhile we hitched on trucks to Smolensk, flying an Li-2 cargo plane from there to Moscow. I should mention that during this retreat we did not ask ourselves why we were retreating. We assumed this was a temporary circumstance – we didn't have time to think about it.

The Li-2 dumped us at Moscow's Central Airfield. Remnants of baffled regiments from Belorussia, the Baltic States and the Ukraine had all gathered there. We were accommodated in a dormitory of the Zhukovski Academy. It was here that we began asking how such a catastrophe could happen: but there were no answers.

Soon a two-squadron regiment was formed and sent to Dyagilevo Airfield at Ryazan, there to receive new MiG fighters. Well, a pilot who can fly an I-16 can fly any fighter. The I-16 is such a sensitive plane: if you push the throttle too hard on take off the plane turns and you can break your landing gear; if you pull the stick a little the plane starts to roll. It was a very manoeuvrable machine but it was too slow. The MiG-3 looked a formidable plane in comparison with the I-16, with an air-cooled engine, a large-calibre UBS machine gun and two ShKAS machine guns. They gave us basic training for MiGs, explaining where the throttle, stick and triggers were, and providing instructions for flying the plane. Then we were told: 'Now, guys, you fly it yourselves.' The plane was very easy to fly. For example, you just had to get close enough to the ground and it would land almost by itself. Unfortunately it was slow as a cow at altitudes of 2,000–5,000m – and most dogfights took place within this very interval. And yet, at altitudes of 5,000–10,000m this fighter was excellent. We were happiest when escorting Pe-2s, which always flew above 4,000m, or when covering ground troops at these altitudes.

But in some cases, alas, we were sent to escort *Shturmoviks*, which flew as low as 1,000–1,200m. I couldn't fly that low – I would have been shot down! I would fly higher, but the camouflaged *Shturmoviks* were not easy to see against snow or forest, so we'd often lose them. Sometimes the Messers would find them before us. Then we'd hear over the radio: 'Hats! Hats! Cover us!' And we'd dive down to their group. Were we punished for losses in the escorted group? No, there were debriefings, during which you might receive an official reprimand. But war is war.

It was easier to escort bombers – they'd fly at 3,000–4,000m. We'd usually fly above them, but sometimes we flew together with them, even making rolls in front of them to cheer them up. Of course, if we came under attack from German fighters the bombers would quickly disengage, almost diving. It was almost impossible to catch up with them later, so we cursed them for that. Another scenario was that their formation would be lost after bombing a target: they'd all fly in different directions and you didn't know who you should cover!

In late August the regiment flew to the town of Spas-Demensk on the Kalinin Front. From that airfield we carried out normal combat missions: reconnaissance, covering ground troops and escorting I-15s and I-153s (which flew ground assault missions) and bombers. Sometimes we had to perform ground assault missions ourselves, and also orchestrated artillery fire from the air.

I should mention that during the first air battles in the Baltic States the Germans forced us to change our tactics. We began the campaign flying in three-plane formations, while German flights consisted of four fighters in pairs. When engaging the enemy our three-plane flights immediately lost formation. For example, at the very first turn to the left, the left wingman had to decrease speed: something completely unacceptable in battle, especially against opposing fighters. Thus every Russian pilot ended up fighting independently, while the Germans remained in pairs – a strong tactical unit. We immediately realized the advantages of the German system and adopted it ourselves.

I recall a well-organized raid by our Air Force on Sescha Airfield. Intelligence had discovered a formidable German task force on that airfield. We knew the Germans always guarded their airfields with fighters, so our flight took off first. At altitudes of 4,500–5,000m our MiGs engaged the German fighters and drew them away from the airfield. Our next wave consisted of Il-2 *Shturmoviks* escorted by a second group of fighters. Their task was to suppress and destroy flak batteries around the airfield. Then the Pe-2 bombers arrived, escorted by MiGs. This third group did not meet any opposition from the ground and bombed the airfield unmolested. As we were told later, a large number of German planes were destroyed at Sescha. Indeed, after this raid the Germans were grounded for several days, which assisted our troops in their successful attack on Yelnya.

On one occasion, Squadron Commander Captain Rubtsov and I were sent to cover our ground troops. At the end of our duty Rubtsov decided to strafe German trenches at the front line, although he had no orders to do so. As a wingman I followed. We strafed the trenches and began a second dive, when all of a sudden, from the clouds, a Messer attacked us. I threw my fighter round to defend us but it was too late: I saw that Rubtsov had been shot down, his plane on fire. We were quite low, so he could not bail out with a parachute. The Germans opened up on me. I escaped into the clouds, but that time I didn't know how to fly in clouds, so I immediately re-emerged. Two pairs of Messers were ready for me. Again I slipped into the haze. I tried my best to manoeuvre but they managed to damage my plane and I was slightly wounded by shrapnel. I imitated a chaotic downfall and – probably low on fuel – they left me alone. I levelled my plane somehow and then the engine stopped. I had to land but where? There was forest all around! I forced myself to imagine that the tree tops represented ground level. I remember seeing one wing fly off, then the other, and then I lost consciousness.

I regained my senses in the cockpit. An old man with teen-agers walked up to the remains of my fighter. They helped me out of the fuselage: 'Come on fella, step forward. Don't even think about escaping.' They treated me like this because a Russian Pe-2 had recently been downed in their area, which the Germans had been using for reconnaissance: so the locals locked me up for good measure. They took me to Babynino village and put me in a barn. I had an awful noise and ache in my head from the impact of the crash. I thought: 'Damn it, I'm in trouble. I should escape, otherwise they'll bring Germans here.' I didn't know on which side of the front line I'd fallen. I sat in the barn a long time wondering what to do. Eventually I decided to escape by making a hole in the roof, which was made of straw. I'd just started when a Soviet NKVD officer walked in and said: 'Don't hurry, pal. You're on the Russian side.' I replied: 'Sorry, I just didn't know where I ended up.' Next day I was back with my regiment, but the regimental staff had already prepared a letter to my family: 'Fell as a hero in the air battle.'

As I had concussion our doctor forbade me to fly and sent me to a hospital, where I remained about a month. When I quit hospital our 10th Fighter Regiment had no more planes left and was removed from the front to receive replacements. On the way to the Reserve Air Regiment in Molotov (Perm) I met my future wife. We kept in touch by letter when I returned to the front, and we married on 3 November 1942, during one of my visits to Moscow.

On 1 December 1941 we were all in the Reserve Air Regiment, where we were re-armed with English Hurricane fighters. It was a piece of junk rather than a fighter. A MiG might be clumsy at low altitude, but when flying higher I felt like a king. In comparison the Hurricane was slow and unwieldy – its wings were too thick. And our fighters had spherical armoured plate, while the Hurricane had straight armoured plate, which was easily penetrated. At first, eight machine guns in the wings seemed formidable armament, but the Hurricane's ammo storage was minimal. And the Merlin-XX engines were bad: they could overheat and jam even if you didn't use engine boost.

Our pilots were incorporated into the 29th Fighter Regiment, which became the 1st Guards Fighter Regiment on 6 December. Meanwhile we'd received replacements from the academies and I became a senior pilot. I ended up in the 2nd Squadron, under Ivan A. Zabegailo.[3] In late December we flew to the front. We were based at Chkalovskoe Airfield, and for two months took care of Moscow's air defence. It was a safe and boring job, while we were all longing for our dear front-line airfields. Finally they transferred us to Migalovo Airfield at Kalinin. We worked in the area of Zubtsov, Karmanovo and Rzhev from that base. In February 1942 we moved to Prechisto–Kamenka Airfield at Kuvshinovo, where the HQ of Gromov's Third Air Army was located. When we arrived at the front we were the only regiment at full strength, with 36 fighters. A sister regiment had only seven MiGs, another just eight LaGG-3s. Starting from 12 March 1942 to

16 April 1942 we had to fly two or three sorties a day. It was hard and we took casualties. By 3 April we only had 13 Hurricanes left.

When the spring mud set in we returned to Migalovo, where the airfield had a concrete runway. Soon Semen Rybalko and I received a mission to cover and patrol the defence line of the Thirtieth Army on the left bank of the Volga at Rzhev. Our time of patrolling was almost over when four Me 109 fighters arrived. For some time we flew parallel to the front line – they were over the German lines, we were over ours. Then they decided to attack. We repelled their assault but the Germans managed to score several hits on my plane. Then the Fritzes disengaged and returned to their airfield and we headed home. But before we arrived I noticed my oil temperature rising. I informed my wingman over the radio (we received radios for the first time in 1942) and he replied that I was trailing black smoke. Our airfield was near but – like an idiot – I decided to overfly it, so everyone could see my plane was damaged. Having flown over the airfield I made a sharp turn and unfastened my seatbelts so that I might bail out. But at the sharp turn my engine stopped! The plane struck the ground with its left wing and crashed – so I was told later by eyewitnesses, for I'd lost consciousness. It took me six weeks to recover in hospital.

In May 1942 we flew off to Saratov to receive Yak-1 fighters. We quickly retrained and flew back to the front. I was shot down for the third time in the summer battles at Rzhev. At the same time I scored my first victory there. We were flying from Sukromlya Airfield in the vicinity of Torzhok. The Squadron Commander led four pairs to provide air cover for the front line. My wingman and I provided a 'hat' at 4,500–5,000m. What's a hat? It's a strike group above the main fighter force. This term came from *Shturmovik* pilots. They would shout to us over the radio: 'Hats, cover us!' Well, I saw the Ju 88s flying in. I warned everyone on the radio that the enemy's group was on the right, then I attacked the Germans. Probably my leader did not hear me or something, but the fact remains that only my pair attacked the bombers, and to make matters worse, my wingman got lost on the way. I shot down one Junkers but came under attack from a pair of Messers: happily they missed. But a second pair of Messers engaged me and one scored a hit on the left side of my fuselage with a high explosive round. My engine stalled. I tried to get rid of them by faking an uncontrolled fall, but alas they followed, wanting to finish me off. All of a sudden two 'Donkeys' [i.e. I-16s – Ed.] from the neighbouring Klimovo Airfield engaged them at about 2,000m. I barely levelled my plane and crash-landed in a wheat field next to Staritsa town. In the heat of battle I didn't even notice my hand was wounded. Our infantrymen ran up and sent me to a medical battalion. After bandaging me they said: 'A truck will be here soon, it'll take you to a hospital.' Why the hell would I want to go to Staritsa if it was under constant air raids? I left, found a road, hitch-hiked, and arrived at an airfield next to Staritsa. They sent me to a medical station there. Two pilots walked in that night: 'Where were you shot down?' – 'At Staritsa.' – 'You know, we rescued a Yak pilot today.' – 'Guys, that was me!' – 'Goddamn it, you owe us a bottle of vodka!' A nurse told us: 'He can't drink!' To hell with all that! Of course we drank together. After several days a plane from our regiment arrived to pick me up. Again the Liaison Officer Nikitin had prepared a letter informing my family of my 'death'. I spent some time in the hospital and went back to the front, to my comrades. I *had* to fight the war. What else could I do? It was boring without my fellow pilots!

Staritsa railway station at Rzhev was used by our ground units all the time. The Germans would bomb it on a regular basis, so of course we had to chase them away. That was the time we first ran into Mölder's squadron – 'The Happy Guys' as we dubbed them. One time a navigator of the regiment flew a sortie, came back, and said: 'You know, these Fritz pilots are different, not just regular front-line units, they have Focke-Wulfs, not Messers.' I should mention that the Focke-Wulf had an air-cooled engine, making it easy for them in frontal attacks. I did not need a frontal confrontation at all: if just one bullet hit my engine I was a goner. So I had to develop a special technique for frontal assaults, steering a bit to the side to avoid the direct line of fire. The same with a bomber: you can't attack it head on because a gunner is firing at you all the time. So I attacked them like this, sliding a bit to the side.

We had a lot of good battles with these 'Happy Guys'. First, we always made a 'hat'. If a dogfight began we agreed that one pair of fighters would disengage and climb higher, observing the situation. As soon as they saw that one of our fighters was under attack, they immediately dived at the attacking German. You didn't even have to hit the German, you just had to fire a burst in front of his plane and he would immediately interrupt an attack. If it was possible to shoot him down we'd shoot him, but the main thing was to knock him out of the attacking position. Second, we always covered each other.

Although the Germans had some weak pilots, most were experienced warriors: but they always relied only on themselves. Of course it was hard to shoot them down, but if one of our pilots failed, a second would come to help him. We came across 'The Happy Guys' again during Operation *Spark*, but they were much more careful then. In general, after Rzhev we were at the same level with the Germans. Our pilots were self-confident. Although the Germans beat us at the beginning of the war, they also taught us how to fight. I must emphasize that we were better motivated and physically stronger.

And yet our replacements were poorly trained and required a long period of adaptation before battle. How did we prepare them? Let's say a young pilot arrives straight from the academy. He would be allowed to fly around the airfield first, then around the area. Finally he would be employed as a wingman. But you could never let him into battle right away – you had to familiarize him with combat flying gradually. The last thing I needed was a flying target for the Fritzes behind my tail! A wingman was there to look after me and cover me when I attacked. If he was struggling to keep up, scared of getting lost, he might easily be shot down. And I would not be able to attack if I had to keep an eye on him: so if a 'green' pilot was in the group, everyone guarded him until he got used to the situation.

One day the Commander of the Third Air Army, 'Hero of the Soviet Union' M.M. Gromov, arrived at our airfield. On behalf of the Presidium of the Supreme Council of the USSR he handed out decorations to distinguished pilots. I was among them, receiving my first Order of the Red Banner. In those early days we rarely received decorations from the government – unlike later – so we wore them all the time, even during battle missions.

In September we passed on the remaining eight or nine Yak-1s to our sister regiment. I led the flight as it approached the airfield. We'd discussed the details of splitting our formation prior to take off. We decided to make a dramatic sharp climb before disbanding with individual aerobatics. We formed a circle over the airfield for landing. Then we lined up our planes on the ground. It was beautiful! I went to the CP to report our arrival and transfer our planes. I ran into an officer at the CP named Colonel Petrov, who turned out to be a former commander of the Chuguevo Academy. After a brief conversation we got into an Li-2 passenger plane and flew back to our airfield.

Next day, personnel from our 1st Guards Fighter Regiment were taken by Li-2 to the airfield at Usman, on the Voronezh Front.

Billeting ourselves in the nearby village, we awaited delivery of our new planes. Two or three weeks later the Yak-7Bs began arriving from the Novosibirsk factory – they had already been test-flown by factory workers. We quickly learned to fly this model, as it was similar to the Yak-1. In fact, the Yak-1, the Yak-7B and the Yak-9 (which I learnt to fly in the Higher Academy of Aerial Combat) were all the same to me. The scariest fighter was the I-16, the rest was peanuts. The MiG fighter would land very easily – you could almost take your hand off the stick. What else can I say about the Yaks? The cockpit was quite comfortable, with a good view and good glass, so we'd fly with closed canopy. In general, the view of the rear semi-sphere depends on the pilot. There was a mirror but you had to turn your plane a bit all the time in order to look around. And you also had to spin your head! You have to see the rear semi-sphere, otherwise you get killed. Sometimes we turned our heads so much our necks were red raw; and when we were flying I-16s we had collar liners of plastic, so our necks actually bled. We had good sights, but there was no time to use them in a dogfight – you'd use tracers from your own machine-gun burst for aiming. Young pilots would press the trigger and fire until their ammo was spent. When they returned, their machine-gun barrels were blue with overheating, so they had to be replaced. If you were experienced you just had to fire a burst, see its trace, get it closer to your target, and shoot the enemy. You can use the sight in peacetime practice. In a dogfight, when each split second is a matter of life and death, you don't care about the sight!

The hardest plane to shoot down? A fighter, of course. The Messerschmitt was a good fighter. The Focke-Wulf was also good but it was less manoeuvrable than a Messer. In general, it all depended on the German pilot inside the plane. The more experienced the pilot, the harder he was to shoot down. Although it was easier to shoot down a bomber, it was difficult to approach a formation of bombers. You had to attack them out of the sun or out of the clouds, or attack simultaneously from all directions: for example, some from above and some from below. In the first attack you had to shoot down the leading bomber, as all other bombers would follow him and drop bombs after him. If you were looking for an individual victory, you had to catch the last in the group. Those were easy targets, as they were normally young, dumb and inexperienced pilots. If such a pilot lost formation and fell behind he was mine! This meant I could count on a 2,000 *roubles* bonus.[4] We would usually pool our money, and if it was quiet at the front we would send a runner to bring us vodka (the usual excuse was to take a damaged plane to the workshop or something like that – I remember that half a litre of vodka was 700–800 *roubles*). With the first burst I tried to hit the cockpit and then shift fire to the wings. You had to save ammo for the second attack – some pilots would spend all their ammo in the first pass and then ram the Germans. No one in our regiment ever rammed a plane. Why? We had good pilots with good training. But sometimes it happened like this: a pilot returned and said: 'I downed a Fritz!' – 'How did you down him if he flew on?' – 'I saw my burst reach his plane.' But when you fired at long distance the burst would bend, continuing behind the target, and while it looked as if the target must surely be hit, the bullets just flew on. When you really hit a plane you could immediately see something like sparks or lightning.

How were air victories confirmed? In general, it worked like this. You returned to the airfield and reported to the regimental CP that you had engaged the enemy, shooting down a plane that fell in such-and-such a sector. If it fell on our territory the ground units from that area had to confirm it. If the plane fell on German-controlled territory the confirmation had to be made by Partisans or by other crews that saw the battle. Were there cases of cheating? We did not have such a habit. Your comrades saw everything. A shared victory meant that I was firing but my wingman was covering me. So I would write that I scored that victory in a group. No one really counted anything. We would put our bonus money together anyway.

After receiving our Yak-7Bs at Usman we relocated to Stary Oskol, where we flew several sorties. But as we met few Fritzes in the air, and our front-line aviation was working well, we received orders to return to the Kalinin Front. We were outraged at first, requesting to be sent to a hotter spot. But the *Stavka* knew the situation better. And so we landed at Staraya Toropa Airfield, where we would soon bump into our old friends 'The Happy Guys' again. Then we were transferred to Zhivodovka Airfield, where we supported ground troops and carried out scouting missions in the Vyazma and Bryansk sectors, and at Lyudanovo, Dyadkovo and Karachev.

At that time workers in the USSR would voluntarily turn in their money to build more tanks, planes and ships for the Red Army. One day I was summoned to the CP with five other pilots of the 1st Guards Regiment. We were handed travel passes for Moscow and ordered to leave immediately, accompanied by the Chief of Staff, Lieutenant

Colonel Kiselev. We arrived at Tushino Airfield and were accommodated in the airfield's dormitory. We were told that several days later we would receive personal airplanes from the Trade Union of Retail Workers of the USSR. While we were waiting I got permission to go to Moscow for 24 hours, in order to meet my beloved little Zina and talk her into marrying me. She agreed and we registered our marriage several days later.

Soon after this my squadron was transferred to the Volkhov Front. We arrived at an airfield near Budogosh town. I should mention that while at the Kalinin Front we did not have a bath for a long time, but in the new place the whole squadron was taken to a steam bath. Next day the pilots couldn't even sit in the warm cockpits of their fighters due to terrible itching: we'd got infected with scabies. To be brief, the entire squadron was immediately out of fighting condition. Our regimental doctor put each pilot on a bench and covered his entire body with some black ointment that smelled like raw oil. Then each of us was wrapped in linen and put to bed. The room smelled like a gas station! The treatment took several days. Before washing us in another steam bath the entire place was disinfected. I should mention that our doctor was quite scared, as it was his responsibility to prevent epidemics, and the whole squadron got sick.

Before our transfer I sent my pay book to my wife so she could get my salary, as I knew Zina and her mother were suffering hard times. We pilots were well supplied with uniforms and food during the war. We didn't lack anything. You cannot feed a pilot on dry bread alone. We young pilots had a great appetite. There were no problems with the supply of fuel and ammo, either. And so all *frontoviks*, as a rule, would send pay books to their wives, mothers, fathers or other relatives, as we knew the food situation on the home front was bad.

Later we moved to the southern shore of Lake Ladoga, to the Valdoma and Kipuya Airfields, where we covered the Road of Life, escorting bombers and *Shturmoviks*. We flew from this airfield from January 1943 till the final lifting of the Siege of Leningrad. There were a lot of our planes in the air, but we didn't come across any Germans at the beginning. Our old friends 'The Happy Guys', flying FW 190s, appeared as late as January 1943. I remember they had the Ace of Spades as their emblem, painted on the fuselages of their planes.[5]

In spring we were transferred back to the Kalinin Front. At night we stayed in a village next to the airfield. After dinner we would spend time with local girls in the club, dancing or singing. We only had a couple of hours for this, as some staff officer would arrive and put us to bed, reminding us we had to fly next day.

In mid-April we were sent to Kuznetsk to get replacement planes. After receiving Yak-7B fighters we flew them to Vydropuzhsk Airfield and then to the Voronezh Front. Again we were at Usman Airfield, near Zavalnoe village. The airfield, which was situated at the village's orchard, was covered with shamrock. But there was a lull in that sector, so we were transferred to Stary Oskol–Novy Oskol. There we flew covering missions for ground troops and carried out reconnaissance. The front lay west of these two towns, and I cherished a dream of asking my superiors to give me a U-2 to fly over the front line to evacuate my mother and brother, who were on German-controlled territory. This dream never came true, as we were again transferred to the northern sector of the Kursk Salient. We flew to Grabtsevo Airfield, where a group of workers from the Saratov plant reinforced the wing surfaces of our fighters, because when we dived at high speed the surface warped. Before the Battle of Kursk began we were concentrated at Zhivodovka Airfield.

On the morning of 5 July I led four fighters on a scouting mission of the Lyudinovo–Dyadkovo–Bryansk railway sector. When approaching Lyudino town we ran into four Me 109s. I shot down two of them and the remaining two escaped. After this successful engagement we took photographs of the railway and returned to our airfield.

I remember the day of 31 July 1943 very well. It was in the afternoon. We had already flown three or four sorties and were sitting in our planes at the ready. All of a sudden a green signal flare was fired from the CP. We started engines, prepared for take off, and were briefed over the radio. Fighters on a scouting mission had noticed a group of about 100 German bombers approaching the front line with fighter escorts. We knew we had a tank corps concentrated in the forest at Lohnya village [in fact the 1st and 5th Tank Corps – Ed.]. Our leadership correctly guessed the German force was flying to destroy our armour. Scouting fighters followed the group without engaging it, which allowed our group leader, Regimental Commander Kainov[6] (I was his wingman) to gain a good attacking position. We met the Germans right over the front line. We approached them from below and the Regimental Commander shot down a Ju 88. I shot down the next one. The escorting Fritz fighters didn't notice our attack and only engaged us when the formation of bombers was already destroyed: thus they couldn't put up an organized resistance. Another group of our fighters arrived and a huge dogfight commenced. To be brief, we completely disrupted their air raid and knocked out a lot of bombers without losing a single fighter.

During the battles at Kursk I scored six individual and three shared victories. After these summer battles I was transferred to the Academy of Air Battle in Lyubertsy as an instructor. I felt offended. By this time I had scored 13 individual victories and six shared victories: I only had to shoot down two more planes to receive the Gold Star ...

How good were the German pilots? Some were strong, some weak. But in terms of morale and physical training we were superior. In fact, much emphasis should be placed on both physical and psychological training. Why psychological training? Because a fighter pilot not only bears the burden of stress in battle, he also bears responsibility for his wingmen, for his comrades. He also has to deal with losing close friends. He must be prepared for all situations, all pressures. For example, I never felt fear before a sortie or during briefing: but sometimes we were navigated by a ground station and I couldn't see the enemy – then I was nervous. I felt blind – the enemy is out there somewhere, probably preparing to attack, but I cannot see him. You go nuts. As soon as you see the enemy your nerves are back to normal. Then all depends on who is stronger.

One time we were escorting *Peshkas* (Pe-2 bombers) at the Volkhov Front and a damaged bomber fell behind on the way back. I sent my wingman to escort the rest of the group and remained with the damaged bomber. He barely made it to the front line before catching fire. The crew began bailing out with parachutes when a Messer appeared from nowhere. He attacked me from behind, fired, missed, and flew past me. We both started turning sharply. My sight darkened from G-forces; I couldn't turn more sharply and neither could he. We were buzzing next to each other in that spin for a couple of minutes. Apparently he'd been scrambled to intercept our group on the way back, so he was short on fuel and disengaged. I also went home. I was left with the feeling that I wanted to shoot him down – and could have – but my fighter was not capable of it.

Were we superstitious? Well, everyone was scared of the number 13 and was unwilling to fly a plane with that number. I, on the contrary, always tried to get a fighter with the number 13. It seemed to me that German fighters turned around when they saw the number

13. In this sense you could say that superstition saved me! But we didn't have superstitions such as not taking pictures or shaving before a flight.

As for cowardice, yes it existed, especially at the beginning of the war. I can remember one pilot was executed in front of his regiment for deliberately shooting himself in the hand. But my squadron never avoided a battle, be there 100, 200 or 1,000 enemy planes, it didn't matter. Why? They can't all attack you at the same time!

But it was hard to lose comrades. There was a young pilot in my flight, Valentin Soloviev, and we were good friends. During one air battle on the Kalinin Front I turned round and saw that he was being attacked by a Messer from behind. His plane was immediately devoured by flames. It all happened in a matter of seconds – I didn't even have time to shout. I couldn't help him and this upset me. I felt bad because I'd lost a friend and because I'd been unable to save him. Of course one gets used to losses – it's part of life at the front. Some people survive, some don't. What did we do with their personal possessions? What possessions?! All we had was a woollen jacket – I never did get that leather coat ...

Notes

1. Lieutenant Eugene N. Zherdij fought with the 273rd Fighter Regiment. He flew 75 sorties, scored four individual and four shared 'kills'. On 14 June 1942, in the Kupyansk area, he rammed a German fighter and was killed. He was posthumously awarded the Gold Star (Hero of the Soviet Union) as well as the Order of Lenin and the Order of the Red Banner.
2. Captain Mikhail M. Karashtin, fought in the Great Patriotic War from October 1942 in the 65th Guards Fighter Regiment and the 976th Fighter Regiment. He flew over 100 sorties and scored at least seven individual victories.
3. Captain Ivan A. Zabegailo flew 453 sorties, took part in 99 dog-fights, and scored 16 individual and six shared victories. He completed his war service in the 54th Guards Fighter Regiment. He became a 'Hero of the Soviet Union' and received the Order of Lenin and the Order of the Red Banner.
4. The bonus for downing a bomber was 2,000 *roubles*, a reconnais-sance plane was 1,500 *roubles* and a fighter was 1,000 *roubles*.

5. The Ace of Spades was the emblem of the 53rd Geschwader, which flew Me 109s and was operating in the southern sector of the Eastern Front. Apparently the author is confusing them with the Green Heart JG54, which fought at Leningrad and flew FW 190s.
6. Major Ilya I. Kainov, Commander of the 1st Guards Fighter Regiment from March 1943 to October 1944, left the regiment for advanced training at the Zhukovski Air Force Academy. He flew 224 sorties, scored five individual and nine shared victories, and was awarded the Order of the Red Banner (twice) and the Order of Alexander Nevski.

CHAPTER TWO

Alexander E. Shvarev

As Told To Artem Drabkin

I met 'Hero of the Soviet Union' Major General Alexander Shvarev in spring 2005 at his apartment in the centre of Moscow. He was very open and willing to talk. The interview ran for over two hours when I realized he was already fatigued. I returned a few days later with more questions and we continued our conversation. The story came out nicely and in April 2006 I invited him to the presentation of the Russian edition of this book but he wasn't able to attend. I later received the sad news that Alexander Efimovich Shvarev had died on 2 May 2006 at the age of 92.

I was born in 1914 and drafted into the Red Army in 1936 as a member of the *Komsomol*. I was sent to the Voroshilovgrad Pilot Academy, from which I graduated in 1939. I graduated on a modern and rather good airplane, the I-16. We had only one squadron flying I-16s, the rest were flying I-15s. After the academy I was sent to Balbasovo Airfield in the Belorussia Military District. It was 1939 and the Polish campaign began,[1] so we (the 21st Fighter Regiment) relocated to the airfield of Lida town, which was then part of the Western Ukraine [i.e. Poland – the town of Lida was absorbed into the Belorussian Soviet Socialist Republic in 1939 – Ed.]. But we didn't have any battle encounters with the Poles and were soon relocated to Kaunas in Lithuania.

I should say that I was well trained on the I-16. Our Squadron Commander was Kutarev, a veteran of the Spanish Civil War [1936–39 – Ed.]. He was not afraid to let us fly and arranged dogfight training on a regular basis. One day he sent me into the dogfight zone. I saw another I-16 entering the zone, doing all sorts of tricks in the air. God knows whose side he was on! And so the dogfight started – a regular merry-go-round. Later it turned out that Kutarev had sent my best friend Alex Viktorov to engage me. In that training fight I beat him up good: I got on his tail and he couldn't get rid me no matter how hard he tried. We flew back and landed. Kutarev told us: 'Great job, that's how you should fight the war!' And so, when our 21st Regiment[2] was rearmed with MiG-1 and MiG-3 fighters, we already had some self-confidence.

I felt comfortable with MiGs. In general a pilot who knew how to fly the I-16 could fly any plane. The I-16 is a very demanding aircraft, very hard to control on landing. First, one has to carefully calculate where to land. After landing one has to make sure the plane doesn't turn to the right or left. Once, as a student in the academy, I went nose over in an I-16. Back then our unit commander was Ageevetski and he flew the I-16 in a bold manner. At that time we were already flying independently and although we couldn't hold direction on the ground, everything worked well. Ageevetski gathered us together before my flight and said: 'Keep in mind that you can tip over on the ground in this plane. If you lose concentration for a moment you'll smash your head!' So I flew my I-16, completed the programme, and calculated the landing. Everything was fine, I was already rolling on the ground. Suddenly I saw the left wing smash into the ground. Next thing I was lying upside down – the plane had gone wing over. I immediately checked to see if the plane was burning but it seemed OK. And so I opened the cockpit door, unfastened the parachute and got out. Standing up I saw a whole crowd of people running towards me. The Unit Commander ran up: 'Are you alive?!' He started prodding me all over: 'You were born lucky!'

Why did I capsize? The problem was that these I-16s were sent from the Far East, worn out after numerous repairs. During the landing I deviated some 10–15 degrees and the left wheel stand cracked from stress and simply folded. The MiG-1 was also tricky to land. Even the Deputy Regimental Commander crashed one. A MiG had a special feature: if you pulled the stick too hard it rolled on its wing. But I didn't have any problems with MiGs.

We continued training in Kaunas: high altitude flights, dogfighting, fire drill at air and ground targets. But we didn't study the aircraft silhouettes of our potential enemy. And yet there were conversations about the war and political officers visited us, telling us the possibility of war could not be excluded. They seemed quite confused by the non-aggression treaty.[3] The Commander of our 31st Fighter Regiment, Pavel I. Putivko, was a veteran of the Spanish Civil War. If someone grew too optimistic about the Germans he would say: 'Keep in mind that the Germans will attack only when they are assured of victory. You have to be very well trained in order to oppose them.' This inspired us and prepared us for war psychologically.

The number of Soviet Air Force regiments grew significantly before the war. The 236th Regiment was formed from scratch in Alitus, and I was transferred as its flight commander. The Regimental Commander was Pavel Antonets, also a veteran of the Spanish Civil War. He was a good commander with battle experience.

We had to fly a U-2 from Kaunas in late June. The place was some 60km from our airfield, so we took a truck with a technician, arriving on Friday 20 June [i.e. two days before the German invasion – Ed.]. The Divisional Commander, who authorized flights, was not in his office. On Saturday we were informed he would be in his office next day. During the night of 21 June I stayed with my friends from the 31st Fighter Regiment. About 4 o'clock in the morning we heard AA guns firing. There had been rumours about a full-scale training exercise, so at first we assumed all was well. But we could see Kaunas Airfield and the meat-processing factory nearby from our house. Suddenly I saw the reflection of flames: 'Brothers, this is no exercise: look, a hangar is burning!'

We quickly dressed and ran to the airfield. No brass hats were present and the hangar was burning. Fortunately we arrived in time to roll the planes onto the runway. Flight Commander Volchok ordered: 'Take off after me!' So we began taking off in pairs. We immediately ran into a group of He 111 bombers – fearsome war machines with strong defensive armament. We attacked and opened fire: but our MiG-3s were armed with 12.7mm BS machine guns, which were prone to jamming – bang, bang, and that was it. The Germans returned fire. After this first battle 40 bullet holes were found in my plane and eight rounds had lodged in my parachute. Can you imagine? A MiG had a fuel supply system, a water system, and an oil system. I was incredibly lucky not a single tube was hit.

The brass hats arrived in the middle of the day and authorized our U-2 to fly, but one of its wings had shrapnel damage. I told the technician: 'Come on, work it faster, we need to fly to the regiment.'

While he was repairing the U-2 we flew to repel the enemy's assaults. In short we flew three more sorties and I scored my first victory. From my first mission I brought only bullet holes but on the second we got smarter. We encountered a single Heinkel bomber and bypassed it from left and right, attacking from both sides. This time my machine guns worked well. The Fritz descended and we followed. His plane was already burning but we strafed him along the Nieman river. Seeing a bridge looming he tried to gain altitude but lost control and crashed into the water. When we returned to base it turned out that my machine guns worked but those of my wingman jammed: so the victory was attributed to me.

Meanwhile the technician was still working on the damaged U-2. I kept asking: 'Is the plane ready?' – 'No.' – 'Is it ready?' – 'No.' Finally he reported that he'd fixed it. I was already boarding the plane and the technician was rotating the propeller when an M-1 staff car drove up. Out jumped Antonets, Commander of the 236th Regiment. His leather jacket was covered with blood: 'Where are you going?' he asked. I was at a loss: 'What do you mean?' But Antonets repeated: 'Where the hell are you going? The Germans are already at Alitus!' If I'd taken off a little earlier I would have flown straight into the enemy's hands. It turned out that on the way to Kaunas Antonets's car came under German infantry fire: the driver was killed but the Commander managed to escape. Only six regimental fighters flew to the Kaunas area, the remaining 25 were damaged and had to be destroyed during the retreat.

The surviving pilots and technicians, including me, were sent to Riga by truck the same day. We drove through the night. Having crossed a river we came under rifle fire: one of our soldiers was sitting in a tree shooting at us. We yelled at him: 'Why are you firing? We're friendly troops!' He replied: 'How should I know if you're Germans or not? I was ordered to shoot so I'm shooting!' Two technicians from our regiment were wounded. That's how our retreat started on the first day of the war. Then we understood the *true* value of our pre-war propaganda, which declared that: 'little blood will be shed, and with one mighty strike we will quickly defeat the invader.' Can you imagine losing a whole regiment of brand new MiGs on the very first day? We were eager to fly and defeat the enemy but already we were losing. We knew we had to retreat but no one was happy about it.

We arrived at Riga but there were no fighter planes for us. Then they gave us I-5s – what a piece of rubbish! We'd never flown them before but we had orders. Several times we flew reconnaissance missions: thank God we didn't come across any Messers! Then we four pilots were sent to Idritsa, where a train of MiGs arrived. They assembled the planes, we tested them, then flew about 12 sorties. I shot down an Me 109 there. A group was supposed to make a sortie. Their Commander told me: 'Take off and cover us!' Several pairs flew off safely but when the last one was taking off I saw four Me 109s. There was no time to think. I flew towards them and opened fire. I didn't see if I hit anyone but the Germans left. I landed and they told me: 'You hit him very well!' It turned out that one of them fell straight onto the airfield. Next day, when we were returning from a mission, we saw our airfield attacked by Me 110s. We were about to start a dogfight but as soon as they saw we were flying MiGs they dived, because MiGs were very clumsy fighters. But I managed to catch one of them. Apparently the pilot was green and fell behind his group. I shot him down. Soon after this an order came: 'Send all MiG pilots to Moscow.'

When we arrived at Moscow Colonel Noga – another veteran of the Spanish Civil War – gathered a group of pilots and we flew to Bryansk in newly tested MiGs. When approaching Sukhinichi I saw that my oil pressure was falling. I thought I could still make it, but soon the engine stalled and I had to make a crash landing. I went back to Moscow and reported to Air Force HQ and they sent me to the Zhukovski Academy, where Antonets, our Regimental Commander, was reassembling the 236th Regiment. When the regiment was ready we were flown to Saratov, where we received Yak planes. These planes were good, and we flew them to Dvoevka Airfield at Vyazma. There was something of a lull in the ground war, but we were flying all the time, chasing away German bombers and performing scouting missions. We also provided air cover for the Front's HQ. During one such mission I shot down an Me 109. It happened like this ...

We were patrolling with four planes. We'd agreed to split into two pairs and circle above the area, flying towards each other. While patrolling like this I looked back and saw my wingman under attack from an Me 109. Even now I can't understand how I managed to turn 180 degrees and make it behind the Messer. I put my entire body and soul into that turn. I looked through the sight but I was so close that the Fritz didn't fit into the aiming circle. I squeezed the triggers of my machine guns anyway and then – whether I shot him down or not – I pulled out, my wingman and the other pair having already returned to the airfield. Then I saw a second Me 109 circling round. I was getting closer and closer to him and finally got on his tail. He dived and tried to escape. I followed. I knew my plane well: I dived, changed the propeller's pitch and got him – the Yak could catch up with a Messer in a dive. I pulled the triggers but the cannon didn't fire and the machine guns were out of ammo. I'd told my technician to shorten the wires to the triggers, as they were too loose, but the bastard made them longer instead! I caught up with the German and even saw the pilot: he had red hair. I wanted to ram him but he hid in the clouds. After this our pilots laughed at me: 'Your red-headed friend is flying up there!' As for the Me 109 I shot down, it fell straight onto the airfield at Dugino *sovkhoz*. How did I know this? When I landed – very agitated and ready to murder my technician – they walked up to me and asked: 'Did you fire?' – 'Yes I did!' – 'We got a phone call, your trophy is lying on the next airfield.'

I shot down another Me 109 at Yartsevo, when we were escorting Pe-2 bombers. We had a dogfight there. I fired at a Messer but didn't see him fall. I never actually saw any of my 'kills' fall. Why? Because after firing a burst I immediately began looking round, in order not to be shot myself! There was no other way. In this particular case my fellow pilots indicated the place where the German dropped. *Peshka* pilots also confirmed my victory.

We barely escaped from Dvoevka Airfield when the Germans broke through the front in October 1941. We were sitting in our planes waiting for orders to take off. The communications were down. The Regimental Commander was walking in circles, very nervous. Then he took the initiative and ordered us to take off. I took off and looked to the right: there was a column of German armour on the road! Thirty more minutes of waiting and we'd have stayed there for good. We landed at Kubinka, refuelled, and started patrolling the area right away.

I shot down the only German scout plane in my whole career then. We took off on a cloudy day, as I remember, and flew to the patrolling area. I saw a plane emerging from the clouds. The Germans had an excellent scout plane, the Dornier 217. I fired all my ammo at him. I fired two excellent bursts but I didn't see if I downed him. I landed and everyone congratulated me: it turned out I did shoot him down. The Political Officer and Commander of the Air Defence Division stationed in Kubinka did their best to persuade me to transfer to their unit: I refused and remained with my regiment.

But our losses were high and we were again sent to Saratov, to get new planes. From there we went to Tushino. When the counter-offensive at Moscow began we were operating from Lake Trostyanskoe, north of Kubinka. We took off on skis for patrolling, escorting, scouting, and air defence missions. The workload was heavy and there were too few planes. I had to fly seven or eight sorties a day. It was hard both physically and psychologically – almost every sortie meant a dogfight. But we were young, and when you are young you take those things less seriously.

And yet some did experience fear. I had Yumkin[4] as my Deputy Squadron Commander in 1943. Once we were flying in formation, Yumkin leading the flight. I had perfect eyesight and this helped me a lot. Having noticed a flight of intruders I announced over the radio: 'A group of planes on the right, 2,000–3,000m above us.' Yumkin immediately became nervous and lost formation: while the rest of us attacked he just disengaged. When this scenario occurred a second time I invited him for a talk: 'Are you fucking scared?!' Yumkin explained he was OK in formation but the moment he heard the word 'Germans' something happened and he became so scared he couldn't control himself. I told him: 'We'll fly together in a pair. If you quit I'll chase and execute you.' I said this in public but naturally I would never have done it. And so we were flying over Krymskaya and this time he held out. When we returned he looked very pale, saying: 'You got me very scared, Commander!' I flew several more times with him and as a result he began performing well.

There was another case in the winter of 1941 at Mozhaisk. Six of us were escorting Il-2s. We were flying through a snowstorm and visibility was almost zero. But somehow we managed to complete the mission and fly back. Sinyakov, an Army Commander (at that time Air Force units were under combined-arms Army control) flew in. Sinyakov was strict, foul-mouthed, and always drunk. He barked: 'Gather the regiment!' We fell in and he paraded in front of us. 'Who fired?' We had eight RS missiles under our wings, but on returning I'd noticed that one of our pilots, Zhukovin, had no missiles left. I asked him: 'Why are you silent? Did you fire?' – 'Yes that was me.' – 'Step forward then.' He stepped out of line shivering. Sinyakov barked: 'You assholes should fight like he fights!' I thought, 'What the hell?!' But Sinyakov said that Zhukovin had shot down two Me 109s with one salvo, and in front of everyone awarded him the Order of the Red Banner. There were shouts of, 'Bravo! Bravo!' Then we asked Zhukovin how it all happened. He said: 'I looked through my sights and saw two planes at once, so I pressed all the triggers. I fired all eight missiles and shot down two of them.'

Soon the good weather set in and air battles commenced. On one mission Zhukovin didn't fly with the group but disengaged. I asked him: 'What's wrong?' He replied: 'The engine is coughing.' But the technicians tried the engine and it was OK. On the next mission Zhukovin said: 'The engine is failing, I cannot fly.' The technicians did another inspection and once again the engine was fine. This story was repeated a third time. But when Zhukovin parked his plane I told him: 'Don't switch off the engine.' I climbed into his cockpit, took off, and performed all aerobatics perfectly. Afterwards I asked him: 'Are you afraid?' – 'No Commander. The engine is not working . . .' Soon after this he aborted a mission in the same way and crash landed his plane. The Regimental Commander had him arrested and put on trial for cowardice. Zhukovin was convicted and sent to a penal battalion.

After the war, when I was studying at the Academy, I'd go to Moscow for the weekend. Walking down the street in uniform one day I bumped into a man whose face seemed familiar: 'Don't you recognize me Commander? It's me, Zhukovin!' My goodness, what a meeting! I said: 'Let's drink a shot of vodka in memory of the front.' As we sat in the bar he told me about his adventures in the penal battalion. As a former pilot he'd been sent with a group of *shtrafniks* to the Vyazma area to hijack a Messerschmitt 109. As it happened they failed to hijack the plane and barely made it out alive. Then they were ordered to take a German prisoner. They captured one Fritz, tied him up, and dragged him off. But they ended up in a Russian minefield: Zhukovin lost his foot and the German was killed. I asked him: 'So how did it compare with the Air Force?' He replied: 'You know Commander, it wasn't so scary in the Air Force . . .'

Of course, at first we feared the German pilots and their experience. When we were at Dvoevka and flew over Yartsevo, I led six planes and a dogfight commenced. It happened that I was the only experienced pilot in the group – all the others were green. We formed a defensive circle. Not a single German approached us! We came back and landed safely. I asked: 'So how was it?' – 'Damn it, they didn't dare to attack our group!' came the reply. I said: 'The main thing is not to be scared – don't care that they are Germans!' A pilot walked up to me and confessed: 'When I see the German crosses

I start shaking.' One had to shoot in battle and his hands were shaking! Later he managed to control his fear and started shooting down Nazis. Confidence comes with experience.

The rule was: if you disengaged without a reason, SMERSh would investigate you immediately. Many pilots were under scrutiny. One case was my friend from the academy, Privalov. He was a bit scared and they wanted to court martial him. But I supported him, as I saw he could defeat his fear. It was never too late to try a person: but he was a pilot so first you had to give him a chance. I took him with me and gradually got him used to combat situations. He did well and finished the war with a breast full of decorations.[5]

Underscoring all this I'd say that in the initial period of the war our morale was affected by German air superiority. In terms of aircraft quality and marksmanship the Germans were better than us. They were flying freely, while we were given specific routes we couldn't change, making us easy targets for them. We only began flying search and destroy missions in the second half of the war. Such missions are the best: you're free to fly anywhere. Your job was to catch lousy pilots and shoot them. In the second part of the war it was much easier in all respects.

Did we consider that we were killing fellow human beings? Not at all. We saw the Nazis bombing our country, shooting and killing. Each of us knew they simply had to be shot down. You fired at an enemy plane as if it were a flying target: especially if you'd developed a desire to score. If you didn't shoot him down, he'd shoot you down – or one of your friends. You had to shoot him first.

Sometimes I even wanted to ram German planes. Of course I'd never have rammed one at low altitude: that would have been sheer suicide. But I remember attempting to ram a German scout at Vyazma in the autumn of 1941. We'd begun a battle and the enemy I was chasing climbed higher and higher. We climbed to 7,600m and I didn't have an oxygen mask (in the heat of battle I forgot to put it on). Four more Russian fighters from Dugino *sovkhoz* joined in and we had to take care not to collide with each other. Now the German pilot had nowhere to go: he couldn't climb higher, meanwhile more and more Russian fighters were arriving. So what did he do? Well, he was obviously very experienced. First he turned 90 degrees, then he shut down his internal engine and dropped like a stone. No one even noticed this – but I did – and dived to catch him. I opened fire when he was completing the dive. Then I saw a burst fired at me and felt it hit home as I was right above him. I approached him at an altitude of 500–600m: 'There you are, son of a bitch!' I thought and prepared to ram him. But as we approached Yartzevo he disappeared into the clouds and that was it. Two scouts escaped me like this. I was very angry with myself.

The second time was when we chased a German scout for a long time – the damn Nazi hit my wingman, jamming his engine and forcing him to land. I continued the chase. I thought: 'Now you'll get it . . .' I saw that the German rear gunner had already dropped his machine gun: that meant he was dead and I could approach without danger. I began my approach but there were clouds at 6,000m and the Nazi escaped . . .

*   *   *

The most difficult sorties? Escort missions were the hardest. A group leader was responsible both for his fighters and the escorted group. He also had to watch out for himself! I flew over 450 sorties, during which I participated in 120 dogfights. From these I scored just 12 individual and two shared victories. They ask me: 'Why did you score so few?' How could it be different? Not only did I have to organize our defence against the enemy's fighters, I also had to lead my pilots, keeping my eyes peeled all the time. I didn't have time to improve my tally and never claimed shared victories.

Escorting *Shturmoviks* was a particularly tricky task. They were camouflaged and were impossible to see against the ground, so you could lose them in a second. I had so many cases when, after an assault, some *Shturmoviks* would fly straight while others veered to the left, and I only had five or six fighters to cover them! In time I got used to this and would put a pair of fighters on the left and a pair on the right. If I had an extra pair I'd put them 100m above, just in case someone tried to attack. But Germans never took unnecessary risks. If they saw that there were planes above they never attacked.

It was easier to escort *Peshkas*. They flew higher and held formation. We'd fly with a pair on the left, a pair on the right, and four behind and above. The Germans wouldn't even try to engage us – even if they spotted us – and we didn't chase them. If you chased them and left the group, you could get into trouble with your superiors.

But there were constant losses in men and equipment. How did we get replacements? When five or six planes were left in the regiment a small group of pilots would stay at the airfield and the others would fly to the rear in an Li-2. For example to Saratov to get Yaks or to Gorki to get La-5s.

As for new pilots, we felt sorry for these young guys. They had five or six hours of flying at their academy. We had to introduce them to battle routines gradually. This meant working on flying techniques like take off, landing and aerobatics. Then we'd train them in dog-fights. After that we'd take one or two young pilots on a mission.

Every experienced pilot understood the new guys had to be taken care of. I had a case near Moscow. We had an airfield with com-pressed snow on it. The Ground Service Commander used rolls of cable instead of special snow-clearing equipment, which he didn't have. He stuffed the rolls with bricks and would roll them all night long. Consequently the strip became orange-red from brick dust. I was ordered to lead the training flights – take off and landing – while my deputy commander took my squadron away for battle training. So we were launching a young pilot from the Ukraine. We took him to the airfield, checked his flying skills, and permitted him to make a circle over the airfield. We told him: take off, make the first turn, the second, then the third, and then you land after the fourth turn. He had everything explained to him. So he took off. He made the first turn and flew God knows where! He didn't have a radio so I couldn't tell him anything. I jumped into a plane, took off, but failed to catch up with him and returned.

Next morning the phone rang. The green pilot called our Duty Officer and reported that he was sitting in such-and-such a place, he was out of fuel but the plane was intact. It turned out he landed on the Volga–Moscow channel, some 150km from the airfield. Can you imagine? We sent Bayandin, a squadron commander, to pick him up. Bayandin was a good pilot but cursed too much. Anyway he flew off, put the young pilot into a U-2, got into the fighter himself, and they both returned safely to the airfield. It was in the afternoon. We sat down for dinner, drank 100 grams, and asked our green pilot: 'How did you get into this fix?' He explained and we almost died from laughter: 'When I took off I climbed to 150m. Then I thought I should make the first turn. I flew for a while and made the second turn: but I could no longer see the airfield. I recalled being told that if you get lost, take a 90-degree course and fly as fast as you can. I flew and looked at the ground. I saw a river. I looked on the map and it said it was the Moscow river, but when I looked at the ground I saw that it was not! I flew and wondered at a long, straight strip. I landed. There was a village nearby. I went to the *kolkhoz* chairman and instructed him to guard the plane. Next morning the villagers and their children gathered, wondering at the plane. I asked them not to touch anything. A U-2 landed, Captain Bayandin got out, and people surrounded him. I reported to Captain Bayandin with all due ceremony: "Comrade Commander, I have landed, the plane is intact, but without fuel. Pilot so-and-so." People were standing around. The Captain told me: "You are a fucking idiot, not a pilot!" The village fed me for a day and it turned out that I was an idiot …' What a story! After that he flew well.

* * *

What constituted a sortie? A sortie was when you flew over enemy-controlled territory or engaged the enemy over your own (we didn't climb above 6,000m, although we had oxygen masks with us, and dogfights normally took place at an altitude of 2,000–3,000m). As for the notion that escort missions were not counted as sorties if the group sustained losses, this is nonsense! But you would be questioned closely if you lost a *Shturmovik*. They would go into all the details during debriefings: what, how and why. A regimental commander would normally debrief his group leaders as soon as they returned from a mission, then he would file his recommendations.

But there were occasions when fighter pilots were at fault. For example, we had a pilot called Lipin. One day, while on a mission, he just turned around and flew away. I later asked him: 'What's the problem? Why did you leave?' He tried to justify himself. I told him: 'First of all you broke our formation, you left your place, you were supposed to be there.' I scolded him. But he did the same thing a second time. After the third time Lipin was beaten up by the other pilots. He started flying well after that. In general such cases of violence were rare. Pilots would take care of these matters in secret, away from the public and the commanders. I only learnt about this beating a week after the event.

* * *

On 8 January 1943 our Fighter Corps Commander, General Eremenko, arrived. I was summoned to regimental HQ and saw the General. Although I was the Regimental Navigator I'd never seen such top brass before, so I felt a bit timid. The Corps Commander told me:

'Don't be shy, tell me what you think of Yak planes.' I told him about the speed, manoeuvrability, and so on. Eremenko pointed to a spot on the map and asked: 'Could you fly a scouting mission to such-and-such a place and see if there is any movement of troops?' They were all afraid the Germans would strike from the south and smash through to their besieged group at Stalingrad. The weather was foul, with clouds a mere 50 or 70m above the ground, but I replied in the affirmative. I flew there alone and looked around. On my return I reported: 'There are just individual vehicles, no concentration of troops.' The General thanked me and flew off.

In the evening they brought a situation report that mentioned a large concentration of German cargo planes at Salsk Airfield – information provided by local Partisans. We were given a mission to scout the situation. I took off in darkness with my wingman Davydov – I just asked them to start a little camp fire at the end of the strip so I wouldn't lose direction. We approached Salsk at dawn. The airfield was swarming with planes. I counted 92 of them. Davydov said he saw over 100. In any case, there were plenty of targets. We flew back and reported the situation. Our commanders immediately scrambled two regiments of *Shturmoviks* from the 114th Division of our corps. I described the position of the German parking slots at Salsk and was appointed leader of the group. I decided to bypass the airfield from the right, fly westwards, and then the *Shturmoviks* would strike the airfield after a turn. And so I flew at 800m while a huge column of *Shturmoviks* followed me at 400–600m. I had to climb from time to time because we were flying over snow-covered steppe, with nothing to help us find our bearings. At first I followed the compass, but when I saw Salsk it was much easier. I steered to the left in order to reach Salsk with a left turn. I led the *Shturmoviks* to the target and they attacked with bombs and RS missiles. At the second pass they opened up with machine guns. That was it. As the Partisans told us later, we destroyed over 60 German planes and burnt a storage dump containing fuel and ammo. In short, it was a classic example of a successful ground assault mission.

When we returned I went straight for breakfast, as I'd flown two sorties on an empty stomach. Pronin, the Regimental Chief of Staff ran up, saying that six Il-2s were taking off for Zimovniki station to bomb a train loaded with fuel and we had to escort them. I said: 'I don't have pilots or planes ready.' In the event we managed to scramble four planes with pilots from the entire regiment. They gave me some crate and I took off, noticing that the radio wire kept coming out of the jack plug every time I turned my head. When we reached Zimovniki the *Shturmovik* leader took his planes into a frontal assault. I knew the station was well protected with flak but couldn't warn the pilot, as I didn't have radio contact with him. The Germans met us with dense flak and Davydov was shot down. But the *Shturmoviks* broke through and bombed the railway track and station building.

Flying back I looked round and saw some 16 Messers chasing us – apparently they were angry after our morning raid at their airfield. By that time the Germans were careful, but when they had numerical superiority they were still strong opponents. We turned around and immediately came under attack. A merry-go-round began. To make a long story short, four Messers attacked the *Shturmoviks*, four more attacked a pair of our fighters, and four attacked me. So I danced with these guys. But the Yak is such a plane that I'm still in love with it! I could fire at one enemy plane when I was under attack, turn, and easily get on the tail of the plane that had just attacked me. I shot down two Germans. I continued dancing with the two remaining Me 109s but saw I had no fuel. Under attack from behind I tried to make a battle turn but my engine stalled and I attempted a landing. I saw a Nazi attacking me from behind. I evaded him by sliding to the side. He fired a burst when I was already levelling the plane, but the tracer flew to the right from me. The second burst also missed. I landed on the belly but it was easy, as the terrain was even and there was a layer of snow.

I saw Germans diving at me in order to finish me off. Where could I hide? I darted under the engine. One Fritz dived and fired. Then he left and the second one dived and fired. Damn it! I'd needed just a few extra litres of fuel: now they were going to kill me – a fighter pilot – on the ground! Next thing an armour-piercing shell penetrated the engine, hit my leg and stuck there. The pain was unimaginable. By now my assailants had run out of ammo and left. I stood up and saw a carriage containing four men, drawn by two horses. I had my TT pistol with me. I thought I'd shoot myself with the last round. I walked up and heard familiar curses: they were Russians but they could also be German-backed *Polizei*. Fortunately they were Soviets. They drove up and said: 'We saw how they fired at you. It's a miracle you survived.' I told them: 'I need a doctor.' – 'There is a hospital nearby.' We took a shortcut across a ploughed field. The carriage was shaking, as it had no shock absorbers, and the pain was horrible. Nurses bandaged me but didn't remove the round, telling me: 'We're not surgeons.'

They sent me to Saratov in the morning. When a surgeon saw the round in my leg he summoned the hospital Chief. An old doctor walked in, looked at me and said: 'Immediate surgery is needed!' They put me on the table saying: 'Well, you have to take the pain now, it will hurt.' The Chief Surgeon pulled the round as hard as he could and my sight darkened with pain. It took me a month to recover.

When the wound began healing I found out where my regiment was and flew to Zimovniki from Engels. But the regiment had already flown to Shahty and only the ground personnel, busy with repairing planes, remained. Technician Josef, my old friend from 1941 (we flew from Alitus to Kaunas together), was supervising the work. I told him: 'Josef, now tell all the technicians to work on one plane for me. When it's ready I'll fly to the regiment!' They repaired a plane and I tested it in the evening. Next day I was supposed to fly off but couldn't find any maps. Fortunately, fellow pilots from an air defence regiment explained where Shahty Airfield was and I managed to find it. After being wounded I was appointed divisional navigator during my period of convalescence.

Before the Battle of Kursk [July 1943 – Ed.] I was appointed Commander of the 111th Guards Fighter Regiment. We were grounded at Shahty until the airfield dried up a bit and then relocated to Krasnodar. We fought for the Krymskaya Cossack settlement. Typical missions were escorting *Shturmoviks* and covering ground troops.

On one occasion we escorted *Shturmoviks* to Anapa. Two regiments of Il-2s, my own regiment, and our Divisional Commander flew on that mission. They said there was a large concentration of German planes on an airfield, but when no planes were found we were re-targeted to a concentration of German armour. Our Il-2s assaulted the tanks and we headed home, landing at twilight. So the Divisional Commander (who was rather chubby) got out of his plane all sweaty and saying: 'That was a good flight!' But suddenly we saw an Me 109 coming to land. When the Divisional Commander saw the crosses on the wings of the German fighter he ran as fast as he could! But the ground controller didn't lose his head and began firing signal flares in the direction of the landing strip. The Me 109 landed and parked next to us. We all remained at our planes. Of course we felt uneasy, but we didn't run, waiting to see what the Nazi pilot would do. Then the canopy opened and a big Czech pilot got out shouting: 'Brothers, I'm one of yours!' He scrambled down and raised his hands in the air: 'I'm one of yours!' He was a Slovak pilot from Squadron 13 (Slovakei)/JG 52, which was operating from Maikop. There were several cases when Slovak pilots defected to the Soviet side. We reported the incident to our superiors and an Army truck soon appeared to pick up the Slovak pilot.

In 1941 we also had an Me 109 in flying condition at Tushino. I'd started studying it carefully and already taxiing it, when we were relocated. I told the Divisional Commander: 'I can fly the Me 109. I'll study it a bit, then I'll fly scouting missions.' He said: 'Go ahead!' So we studied the plane, launched the engine and tested the gas. We decided to do more training next day. But Corps Commander twice 'Hero of the Soviet Union' Savitski flew in and said: 'I'm taking this plane from you. I'll fly it myself.' You couldn't argue with him! He took off, flew to his airfield, and crashed the plane. After the war, when we met again, I reminded him of this case: 'Why did you take my Me 109 and then crash it?' We laughed.

I remember another incident from our time at Krasnodar. We had a perfect pilot, Isaac Reidel,[6] in our squadron. Once we found ourselves escorting *Shturmoviks* in a complete fog at an altitude of 800m. Inside the fog you couldn't see a thing, but above the mist visibility was 'a million by million kilometres' as we used to say. Reidel's pair was above the main group at the fog level and I was a bit below. As I had good eyesight, I was the first to notice six Fritzes making straight for us from the right. I only had time to shout: 'Reidel, turn!' But it seemed he didn't react. The Germans whizzed past. I don't know if they crashed or not, but the other guys, who were a bit behind, saw them collide.

When we returned Reidel was missing, apparently shot down. The *Shturmoviks* had no casualties but we had one fighter and one pilot lost. Three days later, however, Reidel came back carrying four bottles of vodka, an Order of the Red Banner on his brand new tunic of fine English wool. It turned out he heard my warning at the last moment and managed to evade the incoming fighter. But an Me 109 tore off his wing in the collision and he barely made it out of the cockpit. Luckily he landed on Soviet-controlled territory. The new uniform, the vodka, and the Order he received from the Commander of a ground army, as he landed next to their HQ. Such things happened. He collided but shot down an enemy. I was worried how he would behave – people react to glory in different ways – but he continued to fly well.

* * *

The hardest plane to shoot down? It was easier to shoot down a fighter, but it was difficult to approach one: you had to make a whole bunch of aerobatic manoeuvres to do it. Bombers were harder to shoot down, especially He 111s. To give an example: we were at Gelendzhik Airfield (there is a recreation area there now) and they sent us to intercept three He 111s while they were dropping bombs. I approached one of them from the right (I was flying an La-5) and fired a burst, setting an engine on fire. Then I made a mistake. I decided to dive under the bomber and approach it from the left, not realizing He 111s had a gunner defending the lower part of the plane. I made my descent and the German gunner hit me real good. If I'd been flying a Yak he would have killed me right away, but in this instance he hit my oil system. I was covered all over with hot oil and couldn't see a thing. My wingman told me: 'Commander, you're burning! Turn to the left.' So I did. Then he yelled: 'Bail out!' It was difficult but somehow I managed it.

On my way down I saw there was a storm over the sea. I fell into the waves and it was awfully cold. It was good we had life vests! To be honest, I thought my life was over, but I decided to float on the surface as long as possible. I must praise the Navy: they were not afraid to send a small boat to rescue me, even in such a heavy storm. At one point a wave threw me up and I saw the boat – there was hope! They fished me out but the waves snatched me back again. Then a huge sailor held the railings with one hand and grabbed my collar with the other, hauling me onto the deck like I was a kitten. By that time I'd been in the water for 15–20 minutes and was already frozen. The doctor undressed me and they sent me inside, where I took a hot shower. Then they bundled me up and gave me a shot of pure alcohol. I didn't even fall sick after that ducking. But as you may see, a Heinkel 111 with its strong defensive weapons, capable of firing in almost any direction, was a hard nut to crack.

* * *

My first decoration was the Order of the Red Banner. I received the award in late 1941, having already scored three victories and become a squadron commander. As for how victories or 'kills' were confirmed, this was a complicated matter. I've already mentioned that in almost all dogfights there was no chance of seeing if your adversary fell or not. At debriefings I usually stated that I'd simply fired at the enemy. Did I shoot him down or not? The wingmen had to confirm this – they could see better. You had to consult their reports to tell the exact spot where an enemy fell. They would send an inspector there. If some infantryman confirmed the fall, the victory was added to your tally.

Of course, it was not possible to confirm a 'kill' in this way if a plane fell on German-controlled territory. In such situations they had to accept a pilot's word. We had a corps commander, Golovnya, who got the nickname 'Doubting Thomas'. Bazanov shot down three planes in one battle. Golovnya said: 'I don't believe it. If they all fell on enemy territory you could claim anything.' Bazanov didn't give up: 'Let's fly there, I'll show you where they went down.' So off they went. Golovnya saw those planes and only after that were the victories confirmed.

Were there cases of cheating? Devil knows! We didn't have it in our regiment. Why? Because we were good friends. If someone tried to brag or lie he would immediately be reminded of his place. We had a kind of internal bond. Everyone understood we had to work as a team.

Did groups work together to win a pilot the Gold Star? It could happen. But it was not as if the group was deliberately fighting on his behalf. He would just fly in a group and the group would down a Nazi. Then all the pilots would say, 'Let's give the victory to this guy, let him get recommended for a Gold Star.' Such was front-line friendship. Later this pilot would give a victory to his friend. It was all voluntary. We made such deals between ourselves – normally our top brass wouldn't even know about it.

Pokryshkin[7] said that every plane at the beginning of the war was worth ten later, but it was easy for a celebrated ace like Pokryshkin to score. He was flying just to collect victories, no escort missions, no nothing. He would climb very high and obtain a perfect view. When he spotted his prey he would approach at high speed – bang bang – and then make his exit. When I was in battle training for two years Pokryshkin's wingman (I don't remember his name) was working with me. We were asking him what it was like to fly with Pokryshkin. It turned out that Pokryshkin didn't care about anyone and flew as he pleased, while his wingmen had to guard him. He didn't care if his wingmen got shot down.

* * *

The first time I was shot down? This happened at Stalingrad, when we were escorting *Shturmoviks* to Gumrak Airfield. A flak round entered my cockpit from below. The shell passed between my legs, broke the control stick, and flew out of the open canopy (we kept them open in winter to avoid being blinded by condensation). Then the plane caught fire. My speed was about 500km an hour as we were in a shallow dive at about 400–500m. I unfastened my waist belt – we didn't use the shoulder ones – pushed the remaining part of the control stick with my foot, and was thrown out of the cockpit as the plane went into a steep dive. But I couldn't open the parachute: it was winter and my gloved hands couldn't catch the ripcord. I tore off a glove with my teeth and opened the parachute with only a few metres to spare. Another second's delay and I'd have been killed. Meanwhile one of my fur boots flew off. It was minus forty and windy. There I was, standing in the open with only one boot! An infantryman yelled: 'Get down! Crawl over here!' But I didn't know where 'over here' was. Realizing this, the soldier put a piece of cloth on his bayonet and waved it. I crawled over and was pulled into a trench and taken to the rear. I was wounded in the head by shrapnel but it hadn't penetrated my skull: the flying helmet and earphones saved me.

I ended up in a front-line evacuation hospital. I saw enough blood there! Can you imagine a surgeon walking around all covered with blood, sleeves rolled up and a big knife in his hand? He would walk up to someone: 'How are you brother?' – 'It hurts!' The surgeon would inspect him and say: 'Shave him!' Then he would slice off some flesh and throw it in a bowl: 'Nurse! Bandage him and send him away!' Then he'd take a shot of pure alcohol and go on. They told me he went without sleep for more than 48 hours. It was during the offensive operation – plenty of wounded and no more surgeons. I had to wait 20 minutes before he had time to examine me ...

But to return to July 1943 and the Battle of Kursk. The airfield of my 111th Regiment was on the southern salient and the air battles were tough. Of course the Germans didn't have the same quantity of planes they'd had early in the war, but their pilots were still experts and didn't take risks. If they saw a large group they'd only attack someone who fell behind – shoot him down and quit. But there were serious dogfights as well. As I had not yet recovered from my wound, and leading the regiment took a lot of my time, I didn't fly often at that time.

After Kursk we headed west. Shortly before the liberation of Kiev we were on the left bank of the Dnepr. The mission was to make a panoramic photograph of Kiev from three directions. Do you know what this meant? A camera was put on the side of the fuselage and you had to fly at tree-top level taking pictures. My wingman was Alex Chabrov – a good pilot from Moscow. So we flew to Kiev. We dived from 2,000–3,000m, levelled the planes at 50m, and I turned on the camera. Flak opened up: soon bits and pieces were falling off but they didn't shoot us down. I brought back three or four holes, Chabrov the same. Then we returned to take pictures of the two other sides of the city. We received the Front HQ's gratitude for that.

After Okop we flew to Tiraspol and fought there. Then we advanced along the Polish border. When the Krakow operation commenced we were covering ground troops. Corps Commander Machin was at the front line. I flew over to his CP with eight fighters, but before we arrived Machin contacted me: 'You are now to land in Krakow.' I was amazed: 'How will we land? We haven't packed!' – 'It's OK, they'll bring all your stuff later.' – 'Is there anyone on the airfield?' – 'A forward team, get hold of them.' We came flying in and established radio contact. I asked: 'Can we land?' – 'Yes, you can.' I disbanded my formation and started landing. Immediately I heard a series of explosions: it turned out the Germans knew about us landing and opened mortar fire, two planes crashing into shell craters. Nevertheless, we parked and reported the situation. They were supposed to bring our belongings two or three days later.

We went to stay overnight at a nearby church. A Polish priest welcomed us warmly. He served food and Polish vodka to the pilots. We had a nice supper and a conversation. He invited us for dinner the next day as well. When all the 'moonshine' was gone we wanted more. But where could we get vodka? The priest told us: 'If you get a car, I could go to a distillery.' We gave him a 1½-ton truck. The priest left with our comrade and returned with a whole crate of wines, spirits and liquor. I only sipped some liquor but didn't drink it, as I thought it was disgusting. Next day we flew to our airfield, leaving two damaged planes behind. Two or three days later they reported that those two planes had been repaired. They told me: 'Say, you know everything there, fly over and bring them back.' We landed at night, walked into a canteen, and saw that all the waitresses had been crying, their eyes were red from tears. What was wrong? It turned out an entire Regiment had poisoned themselves with methanol, which they took from that same distillery.[8]

I didn't take part in the Battle of Berlin. I was ordered to go to the Academy for the third time. I resisted for a long time but eventually they said: 'Why are you rebelling? Pack your things and fly an Li-2 there tomorrow!' So I did.

*　*　*

Our daily routine? It varied. For example, when we were on Lake Trostyanskoe, the village we stayed in was 3km from the airfield. There was so much snow that no car could take us there. We had to walk in flight uniforms! We would normally arrive at the airfield at dawn. That meant we had to get up a couple of hours before dawn to wash ourselves and get ready. Then we would drink coffee and walk to the airfield.

On the airfield each one of us walked up to his plane and made sure it was flight-ready. After that we all gathered in a dugout and waited for the order to take off. While waiting we'd normally study our documents or listen to some lecture on equipment or tactics.

In the last years of the war everyone knew very well that pilots had to be trained. For example, how to judge the correct distance of fire in a dogfight. I had experience in this and shared it with the younger pilots. I explained that one had to open fire from 20–25m, when you could literally 'see the rivets'. Of course, when we were in the dug-out, we often just chatted and told jokes. We were forbidden to play cards – it was considered a bourgeois habit – so we played dominoes and chess instead.

In general we felt relaxed before a mission. But when a sortie was announced every pilot would work through the whole series of his actions from take off to target. For example, I, as group leader, always wanted to make sure the group was together when we took off. Then my job was orienteering and observation. Even before the flight we'd agree how to react if we ran into Germans above us or to the left or right. We were never scared when being briefed, but of course we were excited.

A technician would meet you at the plane. My long-standing technician was Georgi S. Tsygankov. He was one head taller than me, a very hard-working and amazing person. So a technician would report that the plane was ready and the guns were loaded. You could ask questions, if you had any. The technician would help you put on the parachute, get into the cockpit, and fasten your seatbelts. Then he'd wipe the glass so there were no marks on it. As soon as you were in the cockpit that was it, you only looked at the engine and all the indicators. Then you'd order take off and the group would fly to the target. After that you'd only think about the mission, how best to complete it.

The maximum number of sorties in a day? In the West and at Krymskaya Cossack settlement I flew seven or eight sorties a day with engagements, which was very hard. As a rule it was two or three sorties a day, and that was OK. For us, our battle day was over with the arrival of twilight. After that there was dinner, 100 grams of vodka, putting ourselves in order. Briefing for the next day also took place in the evening and we'd go to bed immediately after, as we had to get up at dawn.

Sometimes mobile cinema theatres came to show some film. We watched them with pleasure. Artists visited us sometimes, but that was in daytime. Sometimes we had dances in the evenings, where someone would play the harmonica. That was common when the front line was stable and life was quiet. The guys lost no time finding girlfriends. It was a normal life. Even more so that we had girls in our regiment: radio operators, gunsmiths, armourers.

Did we always receive 100 grams of vodka after sorties? Always 100 grams! If you limited yourself to that amount it was a stress medicine. You drink it and forget your problems, you eat your meal and go to sleep. But some couldn't get enough vodka. We had one comrade, for example. He flew two sorties in one day, then went to the canteen with his friends. They drank there, found more vodka somewhere, and it was still not enough. I told them: 'Guys, go to bed.' – 'Yes, yes, Commander.' I left but they stayed. The waitresses asked them: 'Please leave the canteen, we need to clean here!' – 'No, we need more vodka!' Our senior cook was always distributing vodka. He was an old and respected man. He told them: 'Brothers, I have no more vodka.' Those guys got angry and threw the cook into the cauldron. What a shame! They drank too much and lost control. Army Commander Krasovski came next day and ordered the regiment to fall in. He shouted at me and dismissed me, transferring me to the 40th Guards Regiment as Regimental Navigator. But those idiots were not even punished!

The Commander of that regiment was 'Hero of the Soviet Union' Nikolai Kitaev. By July 1944, when he went home on leave, he had over 30 individual victories. At that time my regiment was relocated to Sbarozh in Western Ukraine. The airfield at Sbarozh was on top of a hill. Kitaev came back from leave straight to the airfield. We went to sleep and I briefed him in the morning. Clouds were hanging low so there were no flights. I told Kitaev there was a distillery nearby. He said we had to go there. I wouldn't agree at first, but he finally talked me into it. We went there and were given 100 grams of vodka. I tasted the vodka and put it away: 'I can't drink before flying.' Kitaev drank it. When we returned to the CP the clouds had lifted a bit. Kitaev said: 'Let's fly. I need to report my arrival to the Divisional Commander.' I replied: 'Nikolai, what's the point of flying to HQ? It's only 15km away!' – 'No, we'll fly and I'll report to him.' And so we took off. Our Divisional HQ was on the left, the front line on the right. Something was burning, a pillar of smoke rising up to the clouds. Kitaev announced: 'Let's go, and you can show me the front line.' I agreed and turned around. I flew as leader, he followed as wingman.

We flew along the front line for a while, then Kitaev proposed: 'Let's strafe the front line!' I objected: 'We're at 200m, what's the point?' – 'No, let's do it.' I thought: 'Damn, this is stupid! But he is a hero, a regimental commander, if I refuse he might think I'm a coward.' So I decided: 'To hell with you, let's do it.' We started the attack. I fired a burst. I couldn't see a thing, the air was thick with smoke. We turned around, left the column of smoke, and I asked: 'Kolya, where are you?' He replied: 'I'm at the first turn.' OK. We made the second dive, I went first and he followed: 'Kolya, where are you?' – 'At the second turn.' OK. The third dive. 'Kolya, how are you?' Silence. 'Kolya, where are you? I do not see you! Reply!' I was circling above the place without shooting. He didn't reply. I flew to the airfield where we were supposed to land. I asked: 'Did Kitaev land?' – 'No.' I flew to my airfield and asked about Kitaev. He had not landed there either. I flew back to the front line. He was nowhere to be seen. By now I was almost out of fuel so I returned to base.

Kitaev was a star: even Air Army Commander Krasovski knew him personally. So the next morning a chief of the political section flew in. He immediately attacked me: 'Damn it, you're a coward! You got scared and left Kitaev alone!' I was so outraged that my hand involuntarily rose to strike him in the face. Some officers ran up and separated us. But he was a good guy and didn't report me. When emotions had cooled, I told him how it all happened. He requested a car, took Kitaev's mechanic and some other men, and drove to the front line. They returned late in the evening while we were dining. He entered the canteen, walked up to me and said: 'Alex, I must apologize. You were strafing the front line very well, all the infantrymen are applauding you. They told me Kitaev was shot down by a tank and landed on enemy territory.'

I met Kitaev again after the war. He was chairman of a *kolkhoz* in Belorussia. He told me that when we were attacking he was hit during the third dive and forced to make a crash landing. He was taken prisoner. But the Germans didn't take away his decorations. In fact, they forced him to fly an FW 190 on the Western Front. By his own account Kitaev flew two sorties but didn't shoot anyone, avoiding combat by flying into the clouds. After the war he went through a six-month check, after which he was forbidden to fly.

Much later a former NKVD officer from our regiment, already retired, visited me. We dined and drank together. He told me that when on leave, Kitaev was recruited by the NKVD and given a mission to get himself captured. The idea was that Kitaev should cooperate with the enemy in order to inform our troops about the situation in the Luftwaffe. I didn't believe him: 'It cannot be that a "Hero of the Soviet Union" would let the Germans shoot him down. And Kitaev made a crash landing with only a slight chance of survival.' Later our Divisional Commander confirmed that Kitaev indeed had such a mission. That explains why he kept all his decorations intact and why he only spent six months in an NKVD camp, although he actively cooperated with the Germans.

*   *   *

Did we drink before flights? It happened sometimes. I will tell you of several cases. I only drank once before a flight when we received replacement planes. I felt so sick during that flight! I knew what I was doing and flew well, but I didn't have any concentration. After this I didn't drink a single drop of alcohol before a flight and forbade other pilots to drink, if they tried to.

Another case occurred when Golovnya gave me a mission to pick up 12 La-5s from an airfield at Peryatin, some 60km north of our base at Pereslavl-Hmelicki. Among our group of 12 pilots was 'Hero of the Soviet Union' Ivan Novozhilov. He had a special feature: if he flew sober he was a chicken not a pilot. If he flew drunk he was a great fighter pilot. So we stayed overnight in Peryatin and everything seemed OK. We received the planes and I let the first four take off, then the second, and led the last four myself.

Upon returning to our airfield I asked: 'Has everyone landed?' No, only Gorelov's flight had arrived. I asked about Novoshilov but he was nowhere to be seen. The airfield at Pereslavl-Hmelicki had trees 30–40m high between the field and the road, and you had to land just on those trees. Suddenly we saw Novozhilov's flight coming in with Novozhilov bringing up the rear. He was about to land but decided to fly very low, amazing the crowd. Then he noticed the trees, pulled the stick too hard, and fell into a spin – bang! I thought that was the end of 'Hero of the Soviet Union' Novozhilov. But a postman found him alive: 'I saw him lying upside down, making noises. When I questioned him he didn't reply. I took an iron rod and broke the glass. I pulled him out and an ambulance arrived. He had blood coming from his mouth. They took him away ...'

The guys went to visit Novoshilov in the evening but the doctor reported he was unconscious. Next day we went to visit him again with our commissar. Novozhilov was already moving his hands and trying to speak. The doctor said he'd suffered bad concussion and loss of consciousness. Novozhilov gathered all his strength and shouted: 'Nurse, give me vodka!' They couldn't give him vodka, of course, but gave him a glass of water. He gulped it down and said: 'Good vodka, but a bit weak.' Such a story! He was the only one who drank before flights. But that time he drank too much and crashed. He survived but never flew again.

* * *

The aircraft I flew? I started on MiGs, then switched to Yaks, and then moved on to the La-5 and La-7. It's hard to say which plane was better because they all had their strengths and weaknesses. For example, a MiG was perfect at altitudes of 4,000m and above. But at lower altitudes it was, as they say, 'a cow'. That was the first weakness. The second was its armament: weapons failure dogged this aircraft. The third weakness was its gunsights, which were inaccurate: that's why we closed in as much as we could and fired point blank.

The Yak was a light, manoeuvrable plane. You could turn it around as you pleased. How many times did I manage to escape unscathed from Germans who were sure they'd shoot me down! But in 1941 we flew with skis and this seriously lowered the Yak's manoeuvrability.

The La-5 was also manoeuvrable and on a par with the FW 190. It had a star-shaped air-cooled engine, which protected you in frontal attacks. The La-5 had good protection and armour in front, so you could engage Heinkels head on without fear. But visibility – especially frontal observation – was worse than on a Yak. Yet we learnt to manoeuvre the plane.

If we compare weapons, there were different options. Yaks mostly had a 20mm gun and two machine guns. An La-5 normally had a 20mm gun and two machine guns – that was quite enough. The La-7, in turn, had two 20mm guns. I was the first to receive ten La-7s at Gorki automobile plant and take them to Zheshuv. It was a master-piece of a plane! I also flew the La-5FN with reinforced engine – another good plane.

*   *   *

The difference between Russian and German pilots? Of course the Germans had more experience and better training. We could sense this, especially in the early part of the war. When they'd beaten us up we concentrated more and began hitting back. Then they became very careful, only attacking when they saw a clear advantage. By the end of the war many German aces were dead and we came across 'losers' as we called them. They didn't have the skills of the aces and we beat them up good.

Did we have superstitions? Some did. For example, some pilots wouldn't shave in the evening. But I wasn't superstitious: it was more convenient for me to shave in the evening! Some were scared of the number 13. I didn't believe this stuff and told them: 'Forget this nonsense!' In fact, if some pilot refused to fly on the 13th, I would take that mission! As a rule everything went well on that date. As for good luck charms, Deputy Regimental Commander Katsin flew with his dog named Tuzik. It was a ferocious mutt – God forbid touching Katsin's map case!

Were pilots ever executed in the air after bailing out? Yes, Sergei Belousov was killed that way. How did it happen? I was a bit lame after Stalingrad so they didn't send me on many missions. Sergei told me before his flight: 'Alex, I really don't feel like flying this mission. My heart says "Don't go!".' But he took off. As other pilots told me afterwards, they ran into He 111s. Sergei hit one of them and it caught fire. But Sergei was shot down by the bomber's gunners. He bailed out and opened his parachute, but German pilots shot him in the air. I never saw our pilots perform such executions. But, you know, some of our pilots bailed out several times and survived. For example, Sergei Gorelov bailed out many times. He'd return, smile, get a new plane and keep on flying. Of course, most flyers were stressed by the experience of being shot down: some got scared and tried to evade dogfights; others became more aggressive. When I was shot down for the first time I didn't get angry but more determined and goal-oriented. I decided to fight till the end. I became a 'berserker' as one could say.

As for the war, I still see it in dreams. Can you understand? All those briefings and battles. And all my friends – those who were killed back then and those who are departing this life now ...

Notes

1. In accordance with the Nazi–Soviet Pact of August 1939 the Red Army invaded Poland on 17 September, the Germans having invaded on 1 September.
2. After receiving new equipment the regiment's number changed from 21st to 31st.
3. Signed by Molotov for the Soviets and Ribbentrop for the Germans, the Nazi–Soviet Pact appeared to guarantee the security of Stalin's western frontier – an illusion shattered by the German invasion of June 1941.
4. Senior Lieutenant Alexander I. Yumkin scored eight individual victories and one shared victory. He ended the war in the 111th Guards Fighter Regiment and was awarded the Order of the Red Banner and the Order of the Great Patriotic War, 1st Class.
5. Konstantin A. Privalov ended the war with one individual victory.
6. Senior Lieutenant Isaac D. Reidel flew 263 sorties, scored ten individual and one shared victory in 57 dogfights. He flew in the 112th Guards Fighter Regiment and was awarded the Order of the Red Banner (twice) and the Order of the Great Patriotic War 1st Class.
7. Pokryshkin, Alexander Ivanovich (1913–95). The son of a peasant who rose to become three times 'Hero of the Soviet Union', a Marshal of the Soviet Air Force and the top-scoring Allied ace of the war. Pokryshkin flew over 500 combat missions between

1941–44 but fell out of favour on account of his preference for flying American lend-lease fighters, such as the P-39. Pokryshkin's official number of individual 'kills' stands at 59, although by his own account he downed over 100 enemy aircraft.

8. Apparently this was an incident involving the 91st Fighter Regiment.

CHAPTER THREE

Vitaly V. Rybalko

As Told To Artem Drabkin

It took several months to convince Vitaly Rybalko to give an interview. Even as the meeting was about to begin, he maintained no one in the modern world would be interested in a war that took place so long ago. And yet a few stories were squeezed out of him ...

A rallying cry was heard in the mid-1930s: '*Komsomol* members, get into planes!' Thus it wasn't hard to join the Air Force in those days. I was interested, there was a chance to study, and in Moscow every district had a flying club. I studied at a club in the Sverdlovski area. Consequently, when I was graduating from the 10th Grade in school, I could already fly a U-2 aircraft. I remember having to skip classes in favour of flying lessons but our doorman, 'Uncle' Vlas, wouldn't let us out of school, so I had to jump from a window on the first floor.

As I was under 17 years of age the instructors from Seschin Academy, who were training bomber pilots, wouldn't take me. But in 1940 Sergei Leontiev, a representative of the Borisoglebsk Academy, selected me as a trainee fighter pilot (by the way, when I was commander of the 3rd Squadron of the 122nd Fighter Regiment in 1943, Leontiev came to lead the 1st Squadron).

They gave us UTI-4s at the academy and we made maybe 11 accompanied flights before they let us fly solo. The training period was short – by early June 1941 I'd completed my course for the I-16. New planes began entering service at that time, so an experimental group of 12 pilots was organized to undergo training on MiG-3s. There were no training planes with a seat for the second pilot so we studied the theory, made two or three runs on the ground, then started flying. Take off was the hardest thing: if you lost concentration the MiG-3 would spin around. In August 1941 I graduated from Borisoglebsk as a MiG-3 pilot. I went to the 122nd Fighter Regiment with two other graduates. Both of my friends were killed in the very first days.

What can I say about the MiG-3? It's my favourite fighter yet all my troubles were connected with it. I spent my young fighting years on it but in 1943, when I'd become a solid and experienced pilot, I switched to Yaks. Probably Yaks were better, although it should be noted that conditions had improved by this time and the war was getting easier to fight. But the MiG-3 was a special aircraft. It was designed as a high-altitude interceptor and had a powerful M-35A engine. At low altitudes it flew like a cow – slow and hard to manoeuvre – but at high altitudes it was a hell of a plane!

I had a case in spring 1942. We were taking off from a muddy field at Ramenskoe to escort Pe-2s. We had five pilots left in our 122nd Regiment and about 80 aircraft: so you could choose which plane you wanted to fly. They were rearming some regiments and we received their old MiGs. There were planes with names like 'For the Motherland', 'For Stalin', and 'For the Bolshevik Party'. I would normally fly 'For Stalin', but at that moment it had technical problems, so I was offered two other planes. I remember answering that I would fly 'For the Motherland' but not 'For the Bolshevik Party'. Thank God there was no NKVD officer nearby! But the simple reason was that the latter plane contained heavy radio equipment and I thought it too weighty to fly well.

So we were supposed to escort nine *Peshkas*. But Squadron Commander Romanenko[1] couldn't take off; and while we were manoeuvring on the ground Misha Korobkov[2] overheated his engine and had to land: so I was left alone. The *Peshkas* arrived and I joined them – the only fighter escorting nine bombers. At the edge of Ramenskoe we ran into four Heinkel 113s [apparently these were Me 109Fs, an updated version of the 109E, which some Allied pilots took for the much vaunted He-113 – a plane that never actually existed, being a successful propaganda and disinformation exercise on the part of the Germans – Ed.]. In my view that was the best German fighter ever, but its problem was that it had a water-cooled engine and all the radiators were in its wings. It was enough to hit it with a needle to knock out its radiator. But in terms of flying characteristics it was an excellent plane.

We were flying without oxygen masks at an altitude of about 1,000m (I'd taken mine off as it was useless). I didn't have a transmitter on my plane, just a receiver, so I couldn't tell anyone I was under attack. Well, the German intruders didn't kill me in their first attack, but forced me to engage in a vertical fight as the *Peshkas* quit the scene. I wouldn't say I was an ace, but I was tough, and made them climb to 7,000m without oxygen. At that altitude the MiG-3 was a formidable machine and I was not afraid anymore. Apparently the Fritzes were low on fuel so they left me alone. I didn't shoot any of them, but had they remained I'd probably have scored a 'kill'.

What sort of armament did the MiG-3 have? There were many options, including RS-82 missiles. I once rescued my Commander with those missiles. It was in February 1942 at Maloyaroslavets. We were returning from a reconnaissance mission: Misha Korobkov and I were on the left and Bazhnov was on the right. Our home airfield was near, so we calmed down, relaxed, and flew in a tight formation, almost singing. I turned my head and saw an Me 110 only 15m behind me! In fact there were two of them and they were sure they'd shoot us down. But I saw them a second before the attack and rolled to the side. Misha was an experienced pilot and also turned away, but Sergei Bazhnov was shot down in the twinkle of an eye. I turned around and saw the Germans chasing my Commander. They were about to open fire but I had four RS missiles and launched them all in one salvo. Of course there was a chance of hitting my Commander, but he would have been dead in a second anyway. The Germans immediately turned back but we didn't chase them, as we'd just enough fuel to get home.

* * *

Throughout 1941 we flew ground assault and reconnaissance missions. On several occasions we supported ground troops, but I remember nothing about those missions. Actually, ground assault and reconnaissance were not counted as battle missions for us, as they were not connected with our primary tactical role. If fighter pilots had counted all their ground assault missions they'd have all received at least one Gold Star!

During one such ground assault mission I was shot down for the first time. I don't remember which mission it was, but I do remember the date: 23 November 1941. We were strafing an enemy column at Tula. The weather was foul and the clouds were only 200m above the ground. During yet another dive I heard a snap: the engine coughed and stalled. Possibly the engine failed, but most likely it was hit by flak. I turned back to the front line but I was very low. I saw a clearing in front of me and braced myself for impact. At the very last moment I saw that I was landing on a row of iron anti-tank obstacles, yet it was this circumstance that saved me. The plane would surely have capsized on the uneven field but these iron spikes tore off the wings, while the fuselage skidded over the ground right to the edge of a forest.

At first I was disorientated – all was quiet. Then I heard firing. I quickly unfastened my safety belts and parachute, jumped out of the cockpit, and made for the forest, ploughing through deep snow in crazy zigzags. I might not have escaped – I was wearing heavy flying overalls and fur boots – but I came across a brook, and splashing into the freezing water, soon lost my pursuers.

I am a city boy and the forest was unfamiliar. To make matters worse I'd left my compass and dry tack in the cockpit. Cold, wet and hungry, I spent the nights lying low and the days attempting to find the front – getting my bearings from the sound of aircraft and artillery fire. The front line was close and German troops were all around – the roads were full of them – so travelling via the forest was my only option.

Clutching a Nagant revolver and seven rounds I came upon a path near a stack of logs. A German soldier sauntered round the corner straight into me. I shot him in the stomach but he continued to stagger forward. Losing my nerve I grabbed a log and brought it down on his head several times before running away. That was the only time during the whole war I killed a German in close combat.

A couple of times I approached villages, only to come under enemy fire when I tried to enter. At the edge of the forest I saw seven or eight Russian officers, all in winter uniforms, lying dead on the ground. I was only 18 years old and the sight made a deep impression on me. How did they die? Were they executed or ambushed? There was no time to find out: a burst of gunfire sent me scampering back among the trees.

During all those days I ate nothing. Once I tried to eat a mushroom growing on a tree but it tasted bitter. By 5 December I was exhausted. Looking back I think I would not have lived another day. That evening

I collapsed in a clearing by a river and decided: 'When the Germans come I'll fire six rounds at them and kill myself with the seventh.' I'd forgotten one round had already been spent! The moon rose. I saw silhouettes advancing. When they were 20–30m from me I shouted: 'Halt, who's there?' Someone answered in a loud whisper: 'What the hell are you shouting for?' I remember no more. Apparently, when I heard my native language and the stress was over, I fell unconscious.

It turned out that our counter-offensive had begun and the silhouettes were scouts from the leading division. I regained my senses lying on fir tree branches. I immediately asked for food. They gave me just a little. On the very next day, when I was beginning to recover, I was sent to the NKVD's special department and the *Osobnyak* [NKVD representative with powers of arrest and prosecution – Ed.] received me. I told him who I was and where I was from. His first words were: 'So now tell me how you betrayed your country! What is your mission here?' I'd walked so long to the front and been through so much that when faced with such a question I burst into tears. Thus the interrogation was interrupted: amazingly there were no more checks.

As my feet were seriously frostbitten the medics were talking about amputation: but I was young and my body recovered. I returned to the regiment and received several days' leave to visit my mother in Moscow. We lived in a communal flat: two long rings and one short one for the Rybalko family. My mother opened the door and collapsed when she saw me. She'd already received papers announcing my death! I spent a single day with her. Next day I said: 'I have to go' – 'Go, sonny, the best of luck to you.' Those were her exact words.

In 1943, in the Mozhaisk area, I was shot down for the second and last time. Again I was hit by flak. I had to bail out. Once I flew back home by a sheer miracle. I landed and rolled my plane on the ground. Everyone was gazing at me and I couldn't understand why. It turned out I was missing a tail and there was a foot-wide hole in my fuselage. That was also flak. I was never hit in dogfights.

* * *

In 1943 my regiment was incorporated into the 5th Shturmovik Corps under 'Hero of the Soviet Union' Kamanin. But even before this, all through 1942, we were mostly escorting *Shturmoviks*. I must say that when we veterans met after the war, no one ever rebuked me for fighting badly or leaving someone behind for the Germans. I didn't have losses in my escorted groups! That's why we still have good relations with *Shturmovik* veterans. But in our regiment we only had one 'Hero of the Soviet Union', and one more in our sister regiment, while the *Shturmoviks* had 160 Heroes! This is not because we performed poorly or fought badly, but because awards were given according to the number of enemy planes destroyed. But as escorts we *should* have been evaluated according to how well the whole mission was completed: if the *Shturmoviks* successfully accomplished their task that meant we escorts had done our duty. We were based at the same airfield as the *Shturmovik* pilots and after a mission we'd smoke together, curse each other, or praise each other. But those guys had dropped bombs, while it looked like we'd done nothing!

If we speak about tactics, we were bound by our position. If you flew higher and lost concentration for a second, you'd lose your group, and as *Shturmoviks* were camouflaged it was hard to see them against the ground. But I had to fly higher than the *Shturmoviks* because if the enemy approached them I was supposed to attack! We had to use a 'scissors' manoeuvre, passing above the group from left to right and back again. Thus the group would fly straight while we weaved about. Consequently we flew at higher speeds, as we had a greater distance to cover. Sometimes, however, when the target was far away, we just had to stick to them, hanging on their tails to conserve fuel. We really hated long-range missions!

If we saw enemy planes somewhere, we hoped they would not come near. To hell with them! When covering ground troops I was supposed to throw my plane at enemy aircraft – I had to chase them, kill them. But when escorting *Shturmoviks* I was only supposed to repel their attacks. That was the sort of psychology we had! I could not leave the *Shturmoviks*, even when fighting off German attacks. Even if my plane was threatened, I could only manoeuvre in such a way as to protect the group.

How many fighters were deployed on escort missions? It all depended on the situation at the given sector of the front, the composition of the escorted group and its mission. A large group would have a large escort, at least two pairs. If we were based at the same airfield as the bombers we'd plan the mission together. It was often like that – we were part of a mixed Air Force Corps. As a rule, if *Shturmoviks* or heavy bombers were flying from another airfield, they'd pick us up en route to the target. We'd be sitting in our planes at the ready. I remember an incident when we were sitting like this and waiting for a group. The Yak-1 had a light tail and you could easily tip over and hit the ground with your propeller. As a rule technicians would sit on our tails to press them into the ground. All of a sudden a group of our bombers appeared in the sky. I was immediately ready for take off but two pairs not yet parked were waiting behind me. I ordered them to take off, which they did, straight from taxiing. When they caught up with me I saw a technician hanging from the tail of one of the fighters! He tried to climb over, in order to straddle the plane like a horse, but lost his grip and fell to the ground from a height of 50m.

Several times I took part in serious large-scale air strikes. On the eve of the Battle of Kursk, during several days from 5–7 July, our Western Front was delivering strikes at German airfields. Misha Bondarenko, twice 'Hero of the Soviet Union', led 24 *Shturmoviks* – a large group. We fighters of the 122nd Regiment covered his attack on Sescha Airfield with three squadrons. It was on 5 or 6 July we flew to Borovskoi. We prepared very thoroughly for that sortie. The battle group was large – two regiments – consisting of a mixed group of 24 planes. We fighter pilots divided ourselves into a close escort group and a strike group. Squadron Commander Major Tsagoiko[3] with two fighter pairs went first, while I was in the rear part of this formation. I should say that the escorting group's mission included the suppression of flak. When Misha Bondarenko led his *Shturmoviks* into the attack, our Tsagoiko and his wingman went for the flak guns and were immediately shot down. Tsagoiko returned a year later but his wingman simply vanished.

Another example. Some twenty years ago I received a letter from a *Shturmovik* veteran named Kazakov. I couldn't remember who this Kazakov was, but he wrote:

Comrade General Lieutenant, I recall our mission in March 1944 to Proskurov. My mission was to attack the western part of town with my six Il-2s. I was supposed to be escorted by four Yaks, but only you escorted us, the other three left with another group led by 'Hero of the Soviet Union' Gerasimov from the 809th Regiment. I was leading my group thinking: 'Where are you going? You are going to your death!' We *Shturmoviks* considered ourselves suicide pilots. Some 20km from the city we came under crossfire from large-calibre machine guns. When approaching the western part of the city I saw an airfield where Ju 87s were landing, covered by Focke-Wulfs. There were about 20 of them and I decided to attack the airfield. We flew into this inferno, fought off the German attacks, but the situation was critical – especially for you. I headed back towards my airfield and then all hell broke loose. I only heard your voice over the radio: 'Kazakov, don't fly lower than 300!' And then you showed real heroism, attacking the FWs, making a sharp turn back, hiding below us under cover of our rear machine guns, and then again attacking the German fighters. We came home without casualties.

Were we forbidden from counting escort missions as sorties if we sustained losses? I never had losses in my escorted groups! We knew immediately if an escorting pilot left someone behind. There was an episode on a return flight, when the escort group Commander informed the *Shturmoviks* they were flying on the wrong course. The *Shturmoviks* disagreed so the fighter Commander decided to leave them to it. He was court martialled but later received a Gold Star.

Was German flak strong? It depended, but normally the Germans provided good flak cover for their ground troops. I saw three *Shturmovik* squadron commanders shot down by flak in one day. Apparently the Germans used some new weapon and we couldn't understand what it was. We flew in – bang bang – and there were no more shots. 'Hero of the Soviet Union' Vasya Gamayun was killed on that occasion – he'd already been recommended for a second Gold Star.

The situation regarding radio? There was no radio in 1941 and 1942. And even when radio sets were available we didn't use them much. Our top brass even introduced the ranks of 'radio communication master' 1st and 2nd Class. We were supposed to learn Morse code and pass exams, but we got extra pay for this. That's how they introduced us to radio.

Was the MiG-3 difficult to maintain? I don't know. But I do know that our technicians were magicians – my favourite fighter was always ready. Only when there was serious battle damage did I have to change planes. I've already mentioned that I had three planes to choose from in 1942.

How many victories did I score? A total of 14 – not bad for a pilot flying escort missions.[4] As for the most dangerous German fighter, they were all the same.

Notes

1. Major Stepan Romanenko fought in the 122nd and 172nd Fighter Regiments, scoring six individual and two shared victories.
2. Senior Lieutenant Mikhail E. Korobkov fought in the 122nd Fighter Regiment, scoring four individual victories.
3. Major Nikolai V. Tsagoiko fought in the 188th, 122nd and 179th Fighter Regiments, scoring six individual victories. He was shot down by German anti-aircraft fire on 10 June 1943. Initially taken prisoner, he had apparently returned to his unit by July 1944.
4. According to the Central Archives of the Ministry of Defence, Russian Federation, Rybalko flew over 300 combat missions, took part in some 38 air battles, and scored eight individual and eight shared victories.

CHAPTER FOUR

Viktor M. Sinaisky

As Told To Artem Drabkin

I obtained Viktor Sinaisky's phone number through the veterans' committee and immediately called him. He was willing to receive me at his apartment somewhere in the suburbs of Moscow. When I began questioning Viktor it was obvious I'd run into a rare example of a very good storyteller. Fortunately I took enough discs to feed my recorder. Viktor could have talked all day but after three hours his wife interrupted, announcing that – as he was recovering from his third heart attack – I should stop asking questions! Later, when I was working on the Russian edition of his reminiscences, we exchanged phone calls. But sadly he did not see the book, as he passed away in December 2005.

I was born in Voronezh, into a doctor's family. I graduated from high school in 1938 and went to enrol at the Moscow Military Technical University. I made it into the University and studied there till autumn 1939, when new legislation on the postponement of military service came into force and college students were drafted. Many students from Moscow were drafted with me, mostly from technical colleges. Apparently this was the reason for sending us to the Ukrainian town of Zaporozhie, to a school for junior Air Force technicians.

The war with Finland broke out in November 1939 and we embarked on an intensive training programme for radiomen/rear gunners on DB-3F bombers. We had ten hours of class a day. The emphasis was on operating short-wave transmitters with Morse code and firing ShKAS machine guns.

I should mention that we former students had a hard time getting used to the discipline of life in a military school. But the fact there was no discrimination between officers and men helped a lot. We were all Red Army men: the only difference being that some were commanders and some enlisted men. And so, when a woman stopped us in the street and addressed us as 'soldiers', my comrade would reply: 'Mother, we are not soldiers, we are Red Army men. Soldiers and officers were beaten by our fathers and grandfathers in the Civil War.' [A reference to the struggle between the 'Red' Revolutionary forces and the 'White' Tsarist forces between 1918–21 – Ed.] In fact, relations between commanders and enlisted men were almost friendly. We had a Red Army House in our garrison, and once you entered you became a fully-fledged member of the club. It had a gym, a movie theatre, a restaurant and dance halls. When inside the Red Army House we enlisted men could invite the wives of our commanders for a dance or a snack in the café. It was the same in hospital. If someone fell sick and ended up there, the doctor would say: 'Forget that you are commanders or enlisted men: you are all sick military personnel. Everyone is equal here.'

Training in the school was very intensive but the 'old hands' helped us, taking care of us 'greens' and teaching us the tricks of military life. For example, when we 12 cadets first came to the garrison we had to wash the floor of our barracks. There were 120 beds in it, so it was not really a room but a big hall. Of course we took buckets, poured water on the floor, and started washing it with rags. The 'old hands' came in and laughed: 'If you wash floors like that it will take you the whole day.' They called in four more men, and taking sweeping brushes, formed a line to push the water forward. They washed one-third of the hall in ten minutes. 'That's the way to do it!' they said.

They also helped us in marksmanship training. We were bad at that. In the beginning it was very hard for us, because a machine gun shudders when fired and consequently shifts about. It was also hard to eliminate jamming. The ShKAS machine gun had a high rate of fire but it also had 48 ways of jamming. Some of them could be fixed immediately, some could not. One day, when we were assembling and disassembling our machine guns, a sergeant major walked in. He was a veteran of the Winter War with Finland and had returned from the front after receiving a wound. He visited us to see how we were doing. He looked at us with a grin and said: 'You have a long way to go. If you work with the same speed in battle you'll be shot down in the first fighter attack. Why? It takes you too long to fix your jamming!' – 'What should we do then?' – 'You have to fix your machine gun in a matter of seconds. Otherwise you're weaponless.' – 'Well, show us how to do it right!' – 'Jam a machine gun, give it to me, and cover my eyes with a cloth.' He fixed his machine gun before we could say a word. That's how the 'old hands' taught us.

We cadets were lucky – the war with Finland was almost over. In late February 1940 the whole group was divided in two: some continued their training as radiomen and machinegunners, while the rest – including me – were transferred to a course for technicians. We studied the M-25 and M-11 engines. I was always interested in hardware. As an aircraft modeller I was familiar with the various types and designs, and I also knew about engines, so studying was easy for me and I graduated with distinction. But training only lasted a couple of months. To be honest, the only thing I learnt was how to weave metal ropes! I understood engines as well as the instructors, not to mention flight theory. At our first lecture the instructor began with: 'A wing that is flying . . .' Well, we all knew what sort of wing it was and didn't bother the instructor. We were all former students from technical colleges and we didn't need this course – we knew the stuff already.

The 131st Fighter Regiment was formed on 12 April 1940. We were sent there as engine technicians after graduation. I don't know why the squadron's Political Officer, Moses S. Tokarev, chose me. I was not the only Jew to graduate, there were many non-Jews as well, but he chose me and I don't know why. I brooded about this for a long time and found an answer when I recalled how he treated different ethnic groups: 'I only know two ethnic groups,' he would say, 'decent people and non-decent people. There are no other ethnic groups in the world.' Such was this man.

I arrived at the regiment when brand new I-16 fighters were being unloaded, having arrived straight from the factory by train. I goose-stepped up to the man giving orders, announcing that I needed to report to Commissar Tokarev. The Senior Technician said: 'I'm the Squadron Engineer. Tokarev is the big guy in the padded jacket over there. Go to him.' I went there. The Squadron Commissar held the rank of senior *politruk* [political commissar – Ed.]. The head of our school had been a senior *politruk* and cadets trembled at the very sight of him. Even a platoon leader was a 'brass hat' as far as I was concerned and here was a squadron commissar in a padded jacket!

Tokarev observed with interest how I goose-stepped up to him and introduced myself. He shook my hand and greeted me. I was amazed – a squadron commissar was shaking my hand! 'I know that you are Sinaisky,' he began, 'I selected you myself. You see that big blond guy? He's my mechanic Garmash. Report to him, he'll tell you what to do.' Then he shouted: 'Garmashidze, your assistant is here!' I walked up to the mechanic. He was a strong, wide-shouldered man in his forties – very imposing. He looked at me and said: 'What are you going to do here in your overcoat? We're about done for today. Go and get an overall – that's all for now. Report here tomorrow morning.' That's how I began my time under the care of Garmash.

Garmash was a very experienced mechanic who'd fought in Finland, at Lake Khasan, and at Khalkhin Gol. Formally we both carried the same rank – that of sergeant-major (I'd received this commission for graduating with distinction) – but he was a professional soldier and I fully accepted his superiority, learning from him as best I could. Garmash could do anything – literally anything. Although I probably had more theoretical knowledge of an engine's function, I couldn't compare with him in practical matters. And so we assembled our *Ishachok* ['Little Donkey' – Ed.] fighter. Garmash gave the orders and I followed them diligently. He soon realized I didn't brag about my rank and well understood my position. As I followed his orders without making mistakes he started trusting me.

I remember the first time I took part in launching an aircraft. For me – an aircraft modeller and a 'green' mechanic – it was electrifying to be involved in launching a plane piloted by Commissar Tokarev himself. The feeling of excitement reminded me of the time I took my first flight as a passenger on a U-2 at the age of 12. When we were seeing off Tokarev, Garmash looked at me with a smile: 'Why are you worried? Everything's all right. We checked everything!' Tokarev flew his mission, returned, and said: 'An excellent plane. Everything is fine.' That's how my service began.

During peacetime our mission at Zaporozhie was to provide air protection for the Dneproges power plant and the town of Krivoi Rog. Patrolling missions took place every day and training flights began at 5am, unless a squadron was on duty, in which case they were postponed until evening. Duty was divided into Form No. 1 and Form No. 2. In Form No. 1 the pilot was seated in his cockpit and everything was ready. If a flare was fired the plane would take off immediately. In Form No. 2 everyone was under the plane and we could rest for a couple of hours.

During breaks the guys would go for a smoke (I was the only non-smoker) and all would flock around Tokarev. He would normally strike up some conversation, throwing out a topic for discussion. Much later I realized how cleverly he educated us, but so delicately that we didn't even notice. Sometimes it happened like this: Tokarev would arrive in the morning and Garmash would report: 'Comrade Commissar, the aircraft is ready for flight.' – 'I know, I know, let's rest. It's two hours before we're on duty.' Then we'd spread a cover on the ground, lie down, and cover ourselves with his leather coat. Sometimes Tokarev would tell us stories, sometimes he'd simply rest.

From the very first day I had great respect for Tokarev. He was revered not only by the squadron but by the whole regiment. Indeed, I would say he was the soul of the squadron. He was like our father. But there were two matters in which Tokarev was very strict. The first was ethnicity: he would not tolerate any racist remarks on this matter. The second was women. Tokarev was a tall, handsome man, and knew very well that women in the garrison were crazy about him, but he never discussed personal affairs. Furthermore, he wouldn't put up with any bragging from young pilots regarding their adventures with women.

There was one incident – it happened on a Monday – that took place in a smoking room. The regiment was formed from two squadrons that had taken part in the Winter War, receiving replacements straight from the academies. The young fighter pilots came from the Kachinskaya Academy and were all proud of their title: 'Stalin's Falcons'. So there we were in a smoking room, while the young pilots, who had just returned from leave in the city, were discussing their weekend. One pilot began bragging about what he did with a girl: he gave her ice-cream, they walked in a park, and then he took her to some bushes where he had sex with her. He shared all the details. I thought that an interesting scene was about to take place, as I knew Tokarev would not let this go without comment. Everyone was listening with great interest, but the pilot fell silent when he saw Tokarev staring at him: 'Comrade Commissar, why are you looking at me so? You have a strange look. Were my words unclear?' – 'No, your words were clear. The only thing that is unclear is what you are – an asshole or an idiot.' – 'What do you mean, Comrade Commissar?' – 'If you went to a park in your uniform you are a fighter pilot, a heroic "Stalin's Falcon", and a handsome guy. Some decent girl also thought that you're a handsome guy and a decent person. Yet you are talking about her like this here. What are you then? Definitely an asshole! Ah, but if she was not a decent girl, then you are an idiot! Let's see if you picked up some venereal disease: if so you will be court-martialled. So, my dear friend, I don't know what you are, an asshole or an idiot ...'

Our Squadron Commander was Captain Senin,[1] a veteran of the Khalkhin Gol and Chinese campaigns. But he was responsible for flying personnel, while Tokarev was responsible for technicians and all administrative matters. Our Regimental Commander was Kondrat.[2] He was a hero of the Spanish Civil War but I rarely saw him fly. I've no idea what he did, as the squadron commanders were left in charge, but in general the regiment was in poor condition. The airfield was also run down, with no link roads between the hangars and the concrete runway. On 15 April 1941 an alarm was sounded: Yakov V. Smuchkevich,[3] People's Commissar of the Air Force, came to inspect our regiment. According to the manual all 60 fighters were supposed to be ready for take off in 20 minutes. In reality we only managed to bring four planes in two hours! The soil in the Ukraine was so soft that planes bogged down: so men from each of our four squadrons had to carry a plane from the hangars to the runway on their shoulders. We were forbidden to start engines. I remember that the regiment was lined up and Smuchkevich walked along with his stick. Kondrat and the other officers followed. I heard Smuchkevich say to Kondrat: 'The war with Germany will start any time and you think this is just a game?' In short, Kondrat was immediately dismissed.

Lieutenant Colonel Goncharov replaced him. He was not so celebrated a commander as Kondrat, but an experienced, educated officer and an excellent pilot. He brought everything under his direct control. We started flying twice a day. I don't know how he managed this because the Garrison Chief commanded a bomber division, whose pilots also used the airfield and usually got priority for flying time. But in May 1941 – a month after Goncharov's arrival – we relocated to Novaya Poltavka Airfield at Nikolaev and intensive training commenced. Goncharov achieved what Kondrat had failed to do: he trained young pilots – stressing flying in wings – and successfully brought them up to the level of more experienced flyers.

There were many good pilots among our officers, but some didn't understand the seriousness of our situation. I remember that after a training dogfight Senior Lieutenant Sherbinin was studying posters depicting the aircraft of probable enemies. Looking at the German planes Sherbinin selected a Messerschmitt saying, 'It would be nice to engage this one. I would have downed him!' I looked at Tokarev. His face, normally kind, darkened at once: 'What are you to a Messer?' he said to Sherbinin, 'what can you offer to oppose him? You make turns with satisfactory results at best. And your shooting? How do you shoot? From 120 rounds three hits on a cone are satisfactory; up to ten – good; over ten – excellent. You never score more than ten! Sigov[4] scores up to 60 hits: if all of you were shooting like him perhaps you could say something!' But Tokarev was only just starting: 'What can you do against a Messer? A Messer has a cannon and large-calibre machine guns; it's protected by armour and its speed is greater than our I-16s. What can you offer against all that? Enough of this bragging! I'm outraged by this irresponsible talk on the radio and in the movies. War is not a game. "Little blood will be shed"? Let's see how little blood will be shed! We have to learn to fight effectively. We have just confronted Finland. You know that our fighters couldn't down a Bristol Blenheim? So how can you think it would be easy to down a Junkers or a Heinkel? You think there will be morons inside them? German pilots are probably the best in the world. They already have battle experience. What can you offer against all this? Enough of this bragging!' And then he addressed the younger pilots: 'You younger ones should be especially keen. Look around for people to learn from. Learn from Sigov. You know that Sigov shot down five Japanese planes at Khalkhin Gol and forced one of their pilots to land at our airfield? Here is an example for you! You cannot even score more than 10 points in shooting exercise ...'

After that many young pilots drastically improved their performance. The situation was tense, although the media always stressed good relations with Germany, saying that Hitler had not broken any terms of the treaty. Yet somehow we didn't believe this.

On 10 May we flew further south, to Bessarabia. There Tokarev and Garmash lived separately from us in a village, while we all lived in tents next to the airfield. Meanwhile we were in a very silly situation. We saw German spy planes fly over our positions every day, but we were not authorized to oppose them. We couldn't even request them to leave! A Ju 88 would overfly us early in the morning, heading into Soviet territory at high altitude. In the evening he overflew us again on the return flight. Thus the Germans were gathering intelligence, checking what we were doing, and we had to live with it. But on one occasion a pilot took off and chased a German plane. When he returned he was immediately arrested. Strange to say, this pilot was court-martialled in September 1941, after the war had already started.

* * *

The night of 21/22 June was quiet. We spent it under canvas, listening to the patter of falling rain. But howling sirens sounded soon after dawn. 'Not another alarm?' we murmured, 'why won't they let us rest – it's Sunday!'

I ran to the plane, removed the canvas cover, started the engine, and began a systems test. The regiment's four squadrons were lined up on the sides of the rectangular airfield. Our squadron was the closest to the village, so we started engines first. By the time the 4th Squadron started up I'd already finished testing the engine and warmed it up. Suddenly I felt the control handle hit my legs: I saw the weapons engineer pulling the ailerons, indicating that I should reduce throttle, which I did. He walked up and told me to test fire the machine guns. I was outraged because testing four machine guns – taking them off and cleaning them – meant half a day's work and my Sunday would be wasted. He said something else but I didn't hear. Then he punched my shoulder, bent down to my ear, and said: 'Never mind Sunday, Sinaisky, the war has started!'

At that moment Garmash came running. I should say that in peacetime, when we were resting, we would always ask about the battle experiences of the two squadrons in Mongolia. Garmash would say that you had to dig foxholes without waiting for orders: 'If you have a free minute, dig a hole, it will save you. No one will defend you when the bombers come. Even worse, if they start strafing, only a foxhole will save you.' We didn't wait for any orders and started digging in. Then Tokarev came running and we stopped digging, as we had to pull the planes into the nearby forest to camouflage them. By the time a German scout plane arrived there were no signs of an airfield left at all. Apparently this was the reason the Germans didn't bomb our airfield, as the measures were taken in good time. Thus the first day of the war was absolutely quiet for us.

Next day we received an order: two squadrons were to return to the Ukraine to provide cover for Dneproges and Krivoi Rog, while the other two squadrons – the 1st and the 2nd – were to go to Tiraspol and Bendery. Our main job was to cover ground troops in the south and guard the Tiraspol–Bendery bridge. There were unceasing aerial battles around this bridge. Sigov, as one might expect, was the first to score a 'kill'. The trophy fell on our territory and a whole tour was organized to see it. Here was solid proof that German planes could be shot down! But in the first confrontations with German bombers our young pilots realized that 7.62mm ShKAS machine guns were of little use: they fired and fired at the bombers but with no result. To be honest we all became pessimistic. Yet Sigov demonstrated that it was not enough simply to hit a plane, one had to hit its vulnerable spots.

When dogfights over the bridge commenced, Davidkov,[5] Tokarev, Sigov and others proved that one could successfully engage Messers and bombers in an I-16. Even against overwhelming German forces our fighters successfully repelled their raids. The battles were usually over Soviet-controlled territory, so we were able to observe them. The Germans never got to destroy that bridge ...

After some ten days at Tiraspol we were transferred to Pervomaisk. After that we fought in different places: Southern Ukraine, Zaporozhie, Mariupol and so on. By autumn we reached Rostov. It was a fighting retreat and no aircraft replacements arrived: so we repaired damaged I-16s ourselves. Two squadrons had I-16s with four ShKAS machine guns and gas tanks under the fuselage, while two had ShKAS and eight RS missiles.

In July the Germans broke through our defences again. They fed a Romanian cavalry corps through the gap in our lines – a weakened rifle battalion was all we had to send against them. Ground units requested the Army commander to send support from the Air Force. The latter ordered us to operate at will, but to provide assistance to the rifle battalion. Davidkov, who had taken over from the wounded Goncharov as Regimental Commander,[6] sent Sigov as a scout. I remember that when he came back he was laughing and smiling. Davidkov asked: 'What's going on?' – 'The Romanians are marching with a brass band and banners flying. They're marching in columns like it was peacetime! Davidkov, have they lost their minds?' – 'I don't know. They're marching on the open steppe. We will come down on them now! Load RS missiles, I'll lead the attacking force myself!'

Twenty fighters were armed – a total of 160 missiles – and Davidkov led them. They flew in low, fired their missiles at the marching mass, and then continued the slaughter with machine guns. Davidkov returned and another group took off. Our fighters hunted the Romanian cavalry for two days. On the third day we relocated on U-2s and had to fly over this massacre. We couldn't fly lower than 200m due to the stench of rotting bodies. General Lieutenant Korneets visited us later. The regiment stood in formation and he said: 'You have destroyed the 5th Romanian Royal Cavalry Corps. The breakthrough has been eliminated.'

*　*　*

Tokarev was shot down in July. His group was escorting *Shturmoviks* or SBs: the escortees came back safe and sound but Tokarev – who by this time had accounted for six or seven German planes – was missing. Apparently Tokarev's fighters took a beating and his wingman had been killed. But a few hours later Tokarev was brought back wounded in an Emka car. He waved at me and I ran up to him. He pulled out a large knife on a chain and showed it to me. This knife was a gift from his father. Tokarev always carried it, as he believed that one day it would save his life. He guessed right. A bullet from a large-calibre machine gun struck the knife before penetrating Tokarev's leg. If the knife hadn't blocked it, the bullet would have killed him. And so his father's gift saved Tokarev's life. Following this wound Tokarev left to command another fighter regiment. He returned later to become Regimental Navigator for a while; and when Davidkov left for the Air Force Academy, Tokarev was promoted Regimental Commander.

After Tokarev was wounded I had no plane left to take care of, so Garmash and I were attached to a repair base. We were fixing planes damaged in battle. We had enough experience to fix the planes ourselves – which was just as well, because we didn't get a single new plane during our work at the base (they brought us only replacement engines and wings).

The I-16 was not hard to maintain but some of its systems were not well thought out. For example, an elementary thing like an ammo counter simply wasn't there! If you pulled the trigger too long the ShKAS would fire all its ammo in one go and that would be it! At 1,800 rounds a minute it was an insanely high rate of fire. Experienced pilots remembered this but the young ones forgot. A 'green' pilot would come back and yell: 'Damn you! Damn all of you! My machine guns jammed!' – 'You are out of ammo!'

When we finished our repairs and everything was ready the pilot would take off. I always felt nervous, looking at the clock and waiting. In my thoughts I was there with the pilot. Then he would return: 'Everything is fine.' – 'What about the engine?' – 'Everything is fine.' – 'What about the plane?' – 'Everything is fine!' Thank God! The first question was whether everyone made it back. Someone didn't make it? He was your friend, your brother ...

In 1941 the worst thing was the feeling of helplessness. In peacetime the government had convinced us – via the radio and the movies – that we were prepared for war and would not yield a single inch of land. And yet the war began with a long rout from the very first day. This was hard to bear, especially as there was a very real desire to advance at any cost. And it was also incomprehensible. Did we not possess weapons? Did we not know how to fight?

We scored some isolated successes, however. As well as slaughtering those Romanian cavalry columns in the summer of 1941, our fighters also cut up an Italian infantry division. But these were individual cases. What was the general picture in the Ukraine? Well, many Ukrainian units surrendered without a fight. And in the local villages we heard such as talk as: 'Why are the *Moskals* [a derogatory local term for Russians – Ed.] talking nonsense to us? We saw Germans in 1918 – they were normal people!' Even before the war Ukrainians would say: 'The *Moskals* came to eat our white Ukrainian bread!' Meanwhile there were many German settlements in the Ukraine and large-scale espionage was common.

As for the Germans, of course they fought well. In 1941 they were awesome. For example, we'd be defending some town and a message would come: 'Russian soldiers, we will capture this town at such-and-such a time. Do not waste your energy. Surrender! You will not be able to do anything anyway.' Then, as promised, they'd capture the town at the appointed time – bastards! It was a bitter blow to our morale. But when we stopped them at Gisel and destroyed them at Stalingrad, we knew we had a winning hand.

*   *   *

There were several special operations during Davidkov's time. For example, when we were at Pervomaisk the railway station of Bendery was nearby. This served as a junction where the north–south and east–west railways met: trains full of Belorussian and Ukrainian refugees passed through, as did supplies from Leningrad, coming down from the north. During daylight hours the regiment was covering both the station and the railway track, so the Germans couldn't do much. As the regiment didn't fly at night every attempt was made to keep trains out of the station after dusk. But a refugee train arrived one evening, closely followed by freight (fuel, ammo and military hardware) from Leningrad. It was obvious the Germans wouldn't pass up such an opportunity and Davidkov recognized the danger. Thus he, as Regimental Commander, resolved to fly a night patrol himself. There were no landing lights at our airfield, so we decided to use vehicle headlamps instead, and when German bombers appeared about 2am, Davidkov flew to intercept them as Regimental Commander.

Dawn arrives early in the heavens, and as he later told us, Davidkov saw a group of nine bombers against the brightening sky. In rear of the main group came a tenth aircraft, apparently tasked with taking photographs of the bomb damage. Davidkov approached this plane and 'executed' it point-blank. Now the bombers knew a fighter was in the air and they immediately dispersed. But they obviously decided to destroy the intruder, for they circled the airfield, waiting for our lights to guide the fighter home. Now we were in a fix: we couldn't turn on our headlamps for fear the Germans would bomb the airfield; meanwhile Davidkov's time was up and he had to make a landing. Eventually we heard Davidkov approach, reducing throttle, and everyone's hearts trembled. On the ground it was still pitch black. Next thing Davidkov was switching off his engine and taxiing on the runway. We immediately ran to him: 'Commander, how are you?' Davidkov, climbing out of the cockpit, jabbed his finger towards the nearby farmland: 'The corn helped me! I saw the pale corn field and remembered that it bordered the airfield. I dropped my landing gear and made my approach. The corn is 1.5m high so when my wheels hit the stalks I decreased throttle and landed.'

But despite Davidkov's efforts, next day the trains stayed put! Some said the trains had been left as a diversion; others that they had no engines. But Tokarev put it like this: 'No enemy bomber can do as much damage as one of our own idiots. The most dangerous person in the world is an idiot!'

Davidkov flew again the following night. But the Germans were ready for him. When he destroyed a bomber the rear gunner of the next one immediately opened up and Davidkov was shot down. Nevertheless, he managed to crash land near the station, sustaining a slight head injury, and was soon picked up by the *kolkhoz* peasants. But when the farm workers realized who he was – the night flyer who'd downed two enemy planes – they recognized their saviour: so they hoisted him onto their shoulders and carried him all the way back to the airfield. It was a special case.

Another notable episode occurred when we received orders to attack the airfield at Taganrog. The instructions were typical: eight I-16s and several LaGG-3s were supposed to take off at dawn, cross the front line at such-and-such a place, and assault the airfield. Davidkov knew the order had come from above but said: 'We'll be slaughtered before we even arrive. This is no good.' – 'Are you refusing to follow orders?' – 'No. Just give me a mission to assault the airfield and I'll decide how best to do it.' He explained his plan to Goncharov: they would fly at dawn, cross the front at the Sea of Azov – where no one expected them – and approach Taganrog from the sea. Davidkov led the group. They flew at an altitude of 15m, remaining unseen from the seashore, and caught the Germans completely unprepared. Davidkov's group made several passes and destroyed twenty-two German planes on the ground while technicians were working on the engines. Fortunately the German AA guns were covered with tarpaulin. When Davidkov returned the top brass were delighted and ordered him to repeat the raid. But Davidkov objected: 'It won't work a second time – we'll only take casualties.' But orders are not to be discussed and they flew again. Of course Davidkov was proved right: without the element of surprise his group sustained losses.

* * *

What was the attitude of pilots towards technicians? Technicians were highly regarded. For example, in 1941 we were perpetually retreating. Our airfield was on a riverbank. Flying personnel and some ground crew had flown off, leaving a few technicians behind. We'd already packed everything into four or five trucks and were preparing to quit when Kanareitsev, the Senior Political Officer – who knew nothing about the Air Force – ordered us to dig trenches and take up defensive positions. Our armour and infantry had already left: only we were left in the path of the whole German Army. We looked at Kanareitsev and thought: 'Is he mad?' We were thirty or forty men, armed with rifles and pistols and a couple of SMGs – how could we stop the enemy? One German platoon with a heavy machine gun or a mortar would slaughter us! But we did as Kanareitsev instructed.

The worst thing at the front was silence. When it was quiet it meant our troops had left and the Germans were on their way. Our nerves were stretched to the limit. We thought we were doomed. All of a sudden we heard a 'Donkey' flying in. We saw it had a No. 2 on its tail: it was Davidkov, our regimental commander. He landed and strode up: 'What's going on here?' – 'Comrade Major, our Political Officer ordered us to dig trenches to stop the Germans.' Davidkov turned to Kanareitsev: 'You idiot! The whole Southern Front is on the retreat and you're trying to stop the *Wehrmacht* with a handful of technicians? You'll get my men killed! A regiment is strong when it is unified – we are useless without our technicians.' Davidkov ordered an immediate evacuation, adding: 'I'll take off. If the Germans are near I'll dip my wingtips, then you drive away as fast as you can. If all is clear I'll make a circle of the airfield before flying off. Priyuty village is only 60km away. There's no front line any more: German tanks and motorized infantry have broken through. But they've left signallers behind to launch flares and create panic. Don't pay any attention to them! Drive straight ahead and don't stop until you reach Soviet-controlled territory. We will meet you there.' Davidkov took off and made a circle: there were no Germans in sight. And so we drove off, making our way without trouble. Such was Davidkov and his care for technicians!

*   *   *

How did we relocate from one airfield to another? When we flew to another airfield they'd transport us in a Douglas aircraft or a TB-3. Sometimes we travelled in a Po-2 'Maize Cutter' – it varied. I remember flights aboard TB-3s very well. They always put us in the fuselage, which shivered and shook so much, I used to think it would disintegrate any moment. The TB-3 was a mass grave not a plane!

I remember when our regiment relocated to an airfield at the village of Yermaki and was tasked with covering a crossing over the Dnepr. We had no fuel so TB-3s flew in, bringing the necessary supplies. Twenty-seven Heinkels also flew in to bomb the river crossings. They didn't notice our little green fighters parked on the airfield, but they couldn't miss those big lumbering TB-3s: so the Heinkels turned around and came for us! I threw myself at the nearest foxhole but it was already full. The Germans began bombing as I looked about for shelter. It was a long way to the next foxhole, and a wave of explosions crashed around me as I ran, but I made it with splinters whizzing by. Two more explosions shook the earth, showering us with dirt. Then I heard a howling scream, heralding another impact, but it fell beyond our foxhole. That was it – they missed! After several seconds of silence we scrambled to the surface. Incredibly, the Germans had missed the parked planes – both fighters and TB-3s – but my friend Kolya Trandofilov was killed. We buried him without a marker as the Germans could arrive next day.

*   *   *

The hardest plane to maintain? Probably the LaGG-3. It was an unpleasant client! Preparing an LaGG-3 for flight demanded more time in comparison with other planes. All cylinders were supposed to be synchronized: God forbid you from shifting the gas distribution! We were strictly forbidden to touch the engine! But there were constant problems with water-cooled engines in winter: especially as there was no antifreeze liquid. You couldn't keep the engine running all night long, so you had to pour hot water into the cooling system in the morning. Furthermore, pilots didn't like flying the LaGG-3 – a heavy beast with a weak M-105 engine – but they got used to it. There was nothing else to do! But the LaGG-3 was armed with a cannon and Davidkov managed to score some 'kills' on it. Even so, we had higher losses on LaGG-3s than on I-16s. When we received La-5s in 1943 everyone sighed with relief. That was an excellent fighter with two cannon and a powerful air-cooled engine. The first La-5s from the Tbilisi factory were slightly inferior, while the last ones from the Gorki plant, which came to us from Ivanovo, were perfect. At first we received regular La-5s, but then we got new ones containing the ASh-82FN engine with direct injection of fuel into the cylinders. It was perfect. Everyone was in love with the La-5. It was easy to maintain too.

And in 1943 I got a chance to study the Messerschmitt 109 when two German pilots got lost and landed on our side of the front line! One of the pilots shot himself when we tried to take him prisoner; but the second, *Oberfeldwebel* Edmund Rossman, surrendered and cooperated with us while we learned how to service the planes. Six pilots under Vasily Kravtsov were selected by Divisional HQ to fly them. As I knew German, and was a technician, I was attached to this group. The Messer was a very well designed plane. First, it had an engine of an inverted type, so it could not be knocked out from below. It also had two water radiators with a blocking system: if one radiator leaked you could fly on the second or close both down and fly at least five minutes more. The pilot was protected by armour-plate from the back, and the fuel tank was also behind armour. Our planes had fuel tanks in the centre of their wings: that's why our pilots got burnt.

What else did I like about the Messer? It was highly automatic and thus easy to fly. It also employed an electrical pitch regulator, which our planes didn't have. Our propeller system, with variable pitch, worked on oil automatics, making it impossible to change pitch without the engine running. If, God forbid, you turned off the engine at high pitch, it was impossible to turn the propeller and was very hard to start the engine again. Finally, the German ammo counter was also a great thing.

Coming back to the Lavochkin, I repeat that in my opinion it is a perfect plane – very reliable and durable. One time Boris Kozlov[7] was coming in to land and I saw smoke trailing from his engine. What was that? It turned out that one of the engine's cylinder heads had been smashed by a round. A Yak pilot would have been dead, while this guy came back with 13 cylinders working and didn't catch fire.

There were some troubles with Lavochkins but they were not design faults. For example, once we were waiting for replacements. We saw them fly in, engines smoking, and watched them land and park. The Squadron Engineer gave me one of these planes and its 'green' pilot, Boris Kozlov, fresh from the academy. At 22 years of age I was already an adult with two years of war behind me, while Boris was just 20. Although he was technically my superior, he respected me greatly and we had good relations. We remained friends after the war (he passed away recently). So Boris test flew the new aircraft: 'The plane is great,' he said, 'but the engine is rather weak.' And he was right: the engine smoked like a steam train and it was obvious something was wrong with the gas distribution or ignition. I began checking the engine. It was easier to check the ignition so I started with that. It turned out that the ignition lead was installed at the correct angle but in the wrong direction. That meant it ignited too late. I asked who had supplied the planes? Boris answered: 'Oh yes, we were also amazed that the engines don't pull well. But what do you expect? These engines are assembled by kids 14–15 years of age; they could have made a mistake.' I adjusted the engine ...

Boris was a good pilot but I was always worried about him. He was a wingman for Senior Lieutenant Kratinov,[8] a very good and experienced pilot. Once they returned from a mission and I met Boris as I was supposed to. At the end of parking I climbed up on one of his wings and lay flat: one had to guide the pilot, as he couldn't see his way because of the engine. We drove up to a caponier – a covered passage over a ditch – and I motioned that he had to step on the brakes. He waved back that the brakes didn't work. Boris switched off the ignition but we kept taxiing on. We drove into the caponier and cut down the pole that held camouflage net over it, which skewered the plane like a bug on a needle. Thank God no one got hurt! But Titov, the Squadron Engineer – well known for his love of obscenities – came running: 'Damn you, a non-battle loss! I've already reported that all planes came back safely!' I told my pilot: 'Boris, I'll do the talking.' Titov ran up and I told him: 'Why are you shouting? What non-battle loss? A pneumatic system was damaged in combat. What could he do? It is a battle loss.' I asked Boris: 'When is your next flight?' – 'In three hours.' – 'I'll change the fuel tank and the shield. If you need this plane to have eight operational aircraft, I'll fix it.' Kratinov walked up at that moment, and addressing Boris, exclaimed: 'Great job, Kozlov!' Then Kratinov turned to Titov and me: 'He did a great job. He took a hit for me. I was attacked by a Messer and Boris flew in-between us, distracting the German pilot. Great job, brave boy!' Titov shut up immediately. I told Boris: 'You can go, I'll repair the plane.' But Boris felt uneasy: 'I'll help you.' I insisted: 'Commander, go to the CP. You have a flight in three hours – have some rest. We'll take care of everything ourselves.' He replied: 'Yes, Comrade Sergeant-Major!'

I remember another incident with an engine. Kozlov flew in and I saw something was wrong. He was flying the 'unloved' plane. You know, planes are like women: you have 'unloved' and 'beloved' ones. Fighter No. 55 was our 'beloved'. But No. 94 was a bitch that always made trouble for us, steering to the left or whatever. To be short, it was a bad plane and we both disliked it. Boris said: 'This bitch is firing! When we disengaged everything was OK and then – bang! bang! bang! – I thought it was a cannon firing! But no, it was the engine, the first cylinder.' I said: 'How's that? I tested it this morning and it was fine.' The engineer asked: 'How are you doing?' – 'Kozlov says the engine is banging.' – 'Something is banging in his ass! Didn't he engage Fokkers?[9] Maybe that's the reason his engine is suddenly playing up!' I let the engine run for some 15 minutes and then it really started banging like a gun. It was in the afternoon, about 5 o'clock. The engineer told me: 'You can leave only when the engine is working again.' If the engine was banging that meant the gas mixture in the cylinders was poor, but the engine had direct injection. I checked the fuel supply system and everything else. I started the engine and the banging repeated. Then we took off the oil and water radiator – by now this had become a lengthy saga. I disassembled the radiator, washed and cleaned every part, and reassembled it: still the engine kept hammering away. What could I do? I checked all the pipes and the pressure level – but to no avail. It was already dawn and the engine was still broken. Then a very good and experienced mechanic named Grigory I. Bolshakov arrived. He had only three or four classes of school but he was a self-educated technician and a decent guy. He walked up and asked: 'How are you?' – 'Nothing works! I've checked the whole thing. I checked the radiator, the pipes and all.' He said: 'Take every pipe from the fuel system and blow through them or shake them.' So I shook one pipe and something rattled inside. I ran to the regimental repair shop. They were all asleep but I sounded the alarm: 'Get up! Get up!' We took an electric drill, bored a hole in the pipe, and pulled out a rivet without a head. How did it get there? Was it sabotage?

There was another case. I was in the 'front team', which meant that the whole crew was just me and the pilot: no armament specialist, no indicator inspector, no nothing! In fact there was only one armourer for the whole squadron. We'd just changed our airfield and Boris had left for HQ. A truck drove up and brought bombs. They left two 25kg bombs at my plane. The armourer said: 'I'll attach the fuses now and you can hang them on the plane.' It was strictly forbidden to hang bombs on planes with ready fuses, so I objected: 'What, with fuses?' – 'Yes! How can I do the job alone for the whole squadron? You can hang them on with fuses.' At that moment Boris came running: 'Is the plane ready? Germans are crossing some river, we have to fly there immediately, before our Il-2s start bombing it.' I hoisted the bomb on my shoulder but tripped over my long greatcoat and fell. I had only one thought in my mind: 'Not with the fuse!' In my fall I somehow managed to turn the bomb around and it hit the ground with its stabilizer, which bent. I began straightening it and

Boris shouted to me from the plane: 'Leave the goddamn thing! Come here, faster!' I attached the bomb and climbed on the wing to help the pilot. We had to start the engine together, as two hands were not enough. He had to turn on the ignition, turn on the air supply and increase throttle all at the same time. That's why we had to share tasks. He shouted to me: 'Faster, Kratinov is taking off already!' He came back an hour later and parked. I asked him how the flight went: 'We hit them hard! They were cunning bastards, making the crossing under the water.' – 'What about that bomb?' – 'I didn't even see how it fell.' I told him: 'You should have seen your face when I dropped the bomb on the ground!' He replied: 'You should have seen yours!'

Relations between pilots and ground crew were the best one could ever have. The pilots knew their lives depended on us. After the war Boris sent everyone his photo – except for me! He lived in Tula, so I called him: 'Why did you send your picture to everyone but not to me?' – 'Viktor, I didn't have good photo paper. I printed those photos on whatever paper I had. But I couldn't send a photo on such paper to a person on whom my life depended during the war.' In public, however, we followed military discipline and I addressed him 'Comrade Commander' or 'Comrade Lieutenant'.

* * *

Did our regiment participate in repelling the air raid on Kursk? Yes! It happened like this. Our squadron was scrambled to repel a German attack on our airfield (Tokarev commanded our regiment and Kitaev[10] the squadron). A group of 18 Ju 87 dive bombers came: two were shot down – Kitaev claimed one 'kill' and my Commander, Ivan I. Semenyuk,[11] the other; the rest were chased away. Afterwards Kitaev and Semenyuk went to the CP while I remained to prepare the latter's plane. I was just closing the last hatch when Tokarev drove up in a ZIS-101: 'Get in the car!' he shouted. 'What about the plane?' I asked. 'They'll do it without you. Now get in!' I climbed inside and Tokarev continued: 'Sinaisky, you have to help me out. Earlier, when Kitaev reported that he'd scored a victory, Divisional HQ told him that it would only be confirmed after ground units had made their report. Kitaev told them that next time he'd shoot down a German right over Headquarters. Now the German pilots Kitaev shot down are at Divisional HQ and there's no translator.' Tokarev knew I'd studied German before the war.

We arrived at Divisional HQ and I saw the Divisional Commander, Galunov,[12] and all the officers there. Tokarev told them: 'Here is your translator.' They brought in a huge German pilot, about 2m tall. He was a blond and handsome guy. They gave me his flying book. Galunov said: 'Now tell me quickly: where did you fly from and what is your mission?' I translated and the German began his story: 'I am an officer of the German Army and I will not betray the Fatherland. If you guarantee me good treatment, then, after our victory, I will try to advocate for you in Germany.' I relayed these words to Galunov, who immediately grabbed a stool: 'Damn you, bastard! There are houses nearby that you have destroyed. Women are pulling their dead children from the ruins!' Then Galunov smashed the stool down and pulled out his pistol: 'Ask him if he will talk. I will kill him now ...' I asked the German flyer: 'Why did you jump with a parachute?' – 'What do you mean?' he replied, 'I was saving my life.' – 'You thought we would play games here or what? Go on, continue saving your life.' Galunov raised his gun. The German said: 'We flew in with heavy bombs, 500kg, in order to destroy your runway. I flew from Kharkov.' – 'What's your mission for the day?' The German looked at his watch: 'In 20 minutes there will be 500 planes heading for Kursk: it will be a famous air raid. Over 200 bombers will fly over you. The rest will fly in from the north and west.' I translated and Galunov snapped: 'Repeat!' He repeated: 'In 18 minutes there will be 200 bombers here.' Galunov said: 'Take him away. All liaison officers to be brought here immediately. Alert all units. Full readiness for all units – both divisions and the corps. Report to the Front Staff immediately. Inform the superior staffs and inform Moscow. Kursk is in danger.'

At that moment we heard the heavy drone of engines and a column of bombers emerged over the horizon. It was a beautiful formation of silver-coloured bombers. They were closing in, but we couldn't see the end of this 200-strong task force, which was led by a black Condor. Tokarev said: 'Look, they're using night bombers. That means they're already short of day bombers.' The Germans were closing in. We watched our regiment and the 88th Regiment taking off and climbing. Our AA guns fired a salvo and shot down the lead Condor. Next moment our fighters attacked and the AA guns ceased fire. Then our 41st Regiment also took off and a slaughter started. We saw German bombers falling one by one. Soon their formation dispersed and they started turning back. No thoughts about Kursk –

they had to escape! Our fighters chased them. There were 18 Messers – they just looked around, saw they couldn't do anything, and also fled. It was a good show.

Then we saw two Messers and two La-5s chasing them, but not firing for some reason. Galunov asked: 'Who is in the air? What is this circus?' – 'Comrade General, that is Kitaev.' – 'What is this show?' – 'He's chasing the Messers to Divisional HQ.' – 'Well, if they slip away I'll have the bastard court-martialled!' But how could they slip away? Nikolai was master of the situation. One Messer tried to escape: Kitaev hit him at once and the German caught fire and fell. The second German was chased closer and closer to HQ. Almost directly above Divisional HQ the German dived like a rock at 90 degrees and tried to escape, strafing the front line. Kitaev glided, caught up with him, and shot him down.

This was a successful battle. In the Battle of Kursk we lost few pilots but many planes. After three days of battle we had about ten planes left. Volodya Bagirov,[13] son of the First Secretary of the Communist Party of Azerbaijan was killed then. He rammed a Messer above the airfield.

Tokarev was also killed in the Battle of Kursk. He was leading the last eight La-5s in a group escorting *Shturmoviks* and bombers, and was shot down by a pair of German fighters attacking out of the sun from above and behind.

Soon after the Battle of Kursk I was sent on a translator's course at the Red Army College of Foreign Languages. After this I transferred to the Airborne troops. At Vienna I got bad shell-shock and spent a long time recovering in hospital. I lost both my hearing and speech. It was on 9 May 1945 when my hearing returned [Germany surrendered unconditionally on the 7th – Ed.]. They gave me a radio set. I was listening to Radio Moscow in bed and weeping with joy. Later I worked as a translator in the Army of Occupation.

Notes

1. Captain Alexander D. Senin fought in the 131st Fighter Regiment. He flew over 100 sorties and scored three individual victories. He was killed in action in late 1941.
2. Colonel Yemelyan F. Kondrat, a veteran of the Spanish Civil War, was Commander of the 2nd Guards Fighter Regiment. He

flew over 100 sorties and scored 11 individual and four shared victories. A 'Hero of the Soviet Union', he was awarded the Order of Lenin, the Order of the Red Banner (five times), the Order of the Great Patriotic War 1st Class, and the Order of the Red Star.

3. Lieutenant General Yakov V. Smuchkevich was Deputy Chief of the Soviet Air Force and on the Red Army's General Staff. A veteran of the Civil War in Spain and other pre-war conflicts, he was made a 'Hero of the Soviet Union' (twice) and awarded the Order of Lenin (twice) and the Order of the Red Banner of Mongolia.

4. Captain Dmitri I. Sigov fought with the 131st Fighter Regiment, flying 123 sorties and scoring nine individual and six shared victories. He received the Order of Lenin (twice) and the Order of the Red Banner (twice). Killed in a dogfight on 26 October 1942, he was posthumously awarded the title, 'Hero of the Soviet Union'.

5. Colonel Viktor I. Davidkov fought in the 131st Fighter Regiment. He commanded the 32nd Guards Fighter Regiment from July 1943 before transferring to the command of the 8th Guards Fighter Division (formerly the 217th Fighter Division). He flew over 400 sorties, scoring 13 individual and three shared victories. A 'Hero of the Soviet Union', he received the Order of Lenin (twice), the Order of the Red Banner (four times), the Order of Alexander Nevski, the Order of the Great Patriotic War 1st Class and the Order of the Red Star (twice).

6. Goncharov was wounded in July and Davidkov took command of the regiment until his return. When the latter was killed in a dogfight Davidkov became commander again.

7. Lieutenant Boris M. Kozlov scored three shared victories.

8. Major Semen U. Kratinov fought in the 40th Guards Fighter Regiment (formerly the 131st Fighter Regiment). He flew over 400 sorties, scoring 21 individual and two shared victories. A 'Hero of the Soviet Union', he received the Order of Lenin, the Order of the Red Banner (four times), the Order of Alexander Nevski, the Order of the Great Patriotic War 1st Class and the Order of the Red Star.

9. 'Fokker' was sometimes used by Soviet pilots as a colloquial reference to the Focke-Wulf FW 190. But the term is a misnomer as Dutch aircraft designer Anthony Fokker (1890–1939) had no

connections with the company (founded by Heinrich Focke and Georg Wulf) that produced Kurt Tank's celebrated FW 190.

10. Lieutenant Colonel Nikolai T. Kitaev entered the war as a pilot in the 25th Fighter Regiment. He flew with the 40th Guards Fighter Regiment (formerly the 131st Fighter Regiment) from November 1941, commanding the regiment from January 1944. Flew approximately 400 sorties, scoring 24 individual and five shared victories. A 'Hero of the Soviet Union', he received the Order of Lenin (twice), the Order of the Red Banner (twice), the Order of Alexander Nevski and the Order of the Great Patriotic War 1st Class. He was shot down by flak on 19 May 1944 and taken prisoner, but liberated after the war.

11. Major Ivan I. Semenyuk began the war in the 88th Fighter Regiment before transferring to the 249th Fighter Regiment in July 1942. He flew over 300 sorties, scoring 18 individual and nine shared victories. A 'Hero of the Soviet Union', he received the Order of Lenin (twice), the Order of the Red Banner (twice), the Order of the Great Patriotic War 1st Class and the Order of the Red Star (twice).

12. Major General Dmitri P. Galunov entered the war as Commander of the 21st Fighter Air Division before taking charge of the 174th Fighter Air Division. He later commanded the 8th Guards Fighter Division (formerly the 217th Fighter Division) and was promoted to Commander of the 5th Fighter Corps on 5 July 1943.

13. Senior Lieutenant Vladimir D. Bagirov fought in the 40th Guards Fighter Regiment (formerly the 131st Fighter Regiment). He rammed a Messerschmitt 109 in a frontal attack on 5 June 1943 at Oboyan, when repelling a German air raid at his airfield. He was posthumously awarded the Order of Lenin.

CHAPTER FIVE

Alexander F. Khaila

As Told To Artem Drabkin

Alexander Khaila lives near my home, so when I contacted him to arrange an interview he came over. But when he arrived I saw that the short journey had been difficult for him. Physically weak, he nevertheless possesses a strong memory, retaining many facts about the war period. After this first meeting we met again to conclude the interview.

My father was a railway worker, which in those days was prestigious work. When he had a holiday he'd get free first-class tickets. I think his salary was 160 *roubles* a month – a whole carriage of apples cost 80 *kopeck* back then, and meat cost 30 or 40 *kopeck* for a kilogram. We had a good life ...

I graduated from Air Force academy in December 1940, but I'd learnt to fly before this, at a flying club in Shebekino, in the Kursk area. How did I get into the flying club? I was in the 9th Grade and sat next to Kolya Korotkov. He was a couple of years older than me but we became good friends. When we moved up to 10th Grade Kolya told me: 'I'm quitting classes.' – 'Where will you go?' – 'To a flying club.' – 'Do you fly there?' – 'Yes.' – 'This can't be!' I thought he was kidding me. But he gave me a date and time and said: 'Come along! I'll be doing aerobatics in this area.' Still I didn't believe him but it was true! On that day, and at that time, a U-2 plane appeared in the sky and began making turns and loops. In short I realized my friend was flying and became instantly intoxicated. We met and he told me to go to the flying club: 'What tests must I pass?' – 'Loyalty and medical inspection.' – 'No, I'm not going there!' – 'Are you mad? You play for the school volleyball team – you're an athlete!' So I turned up at the flying club, wrote a formal application, and they gave me the 'go ahead'. The loyalty inspection was easily passed: my father was a member of the Communist Party and had commanded an armoured train during the Revolution. I also passed the medical exam, which took place at Belgorod, some 40km from Shebekino. Thus, when I returned, I was officially accepted into the flying club. I studied there for a year and really fell in love with flying.

In 1938 we graduates of the flying club were waiting for a commission from Chuguevo Academy. This commission was supposed to set our final exams. I got excellent grades in aerobatics and was enrolled in the academy, but I had to wait for official confirmation, which only came two months later. And so I ended up in Chuguevo town, near Kharkov. We began flying on a two-seater UT-2, which we used for learning aerobatics and high-speed landing. We did parachute jumps as well. Then the entire squadron of over 200 cadets switched to UTI-4s. After learning to fly this plane, three squadrons – including mine – moved on to the I-16. I made ten successful training flights: but on the eleventh I nearly crashed an aircraft once flown by Valery Chkalov,[1] which we all called 'Chkalov's Plane'.

I graduated from the academy as one of the top cadets and was ordered to remain as an instructor. Thus it happened that I was already instructor while my friends were still cadets, even though we entered the academy at the same time.

I should mention that I graduated as a sergeant. We were expected to graduate as lieutenants – they'd already made us beautifully tailored dark-blue uniforms with a 'Chicken' insignia on the sleeve – but Defence Minister Timoshenko's order came that we would all graduate as sergeants! I was so offended that I never wore the NCO's triangle insignia. To add to our misery we continued to live in barracks, where we were supposed to remain for four years. Of course we sergeants lived in separate rooms, three or four men to each, and were fully provided with uniforms, catering, transportation and so on. But on the other hand a sergeant's salary was 440 *roubles*, while a lieutenant's salary was 750 *roubles*. Thank God they didn't make us shave our heads! In brief, I started my work as instructor in January 1941 and the war broke out in June.

I learnt of the outbreak of war in the following manner. In summer we were accommodated in tents on the airfield. It rained heavily during the night of 21/22 June, and when the alarm sounded no one wanted to get up, as everyone thought it was yet another training exercise. Our entire training process was a series of alarms and they came almost every Sunday. But this time we received an order: 'Everyone gather in the canteen!' We assembled there and waited, not understanding what was going on – especially as we'd already had breakfast! Flights were cancelled, which seemed odd, as training alarms were usually followed by a return to our flying schedule. Shortly before noon they announced a radio broadcast and we heard Molotov's speech. This is how we learnt that war had broken out. Of course we all volunteered for the front immediately, but they didn't let us go. Training continued for several more days. We camouflaged the planes and moved our tents from the airfield into a nearby ravine.

Two days later the alarm sounded again: the Germans had made an airborne landing somewhere near Kharkov. The moon was shining and I saw parachutes in the sky. We received an order: 'Prepare planes for relocation to the airfield at Bulatselovka station immediately.' So we flew there at dawn. Then the air raids started. As a flight instructor I was assigned to a group tasked with repelling the raids. We flew about twenty sorties, but who was counting? Back then no one even thought about it. We fought hard and had a tough time. We flew I-16s against the enemy's Me 109s. German planes were faster than ours. In theory our I-16s could gain 400–450m during a turn, while a Messer would gain 700–750m no trouble. And our gunsights consisted of a simple pipe. What could you see through it? Only the Group Commander had an I-16 fitted with a collimator sight. My friend Valya Firsov, from Orel, was killed in those early battles.

Two or three weeks later we were ordered to fly to Borisoglebsk. It was hard to land as the airfield was so congested. It was full of planes and there were hundreds of pilots. Retreating Air Force units were all concentrated at Borisoglebsk so there was no place to live. We three pilots slept on a two-level bunk in the barracks of the academy.

We expected to be sent back to the front any time. We were wrong. We spent about a month there, drinking beer and going to dances. Dance parties took place every night, regardless of the fact that the Germans were fast advancing into our country. Blackouts, candle light, dances and beer. Only when the Germans approached Kiev did the whole academy receive an order to relocate to Middle Asia by air and rail. That's how I ended up in Chimkent. When our planes were assembled (they were brought unassembled by rail) the squadron was ordered to Jambul, and I continued my work as an instructor there. My former classmates – about four of them – also ended up there. Again I was training them! They didn't fly too well but I let them graduate.

And so I was working in Middle Asia but my heart longed for the front. I wrote a transfer request on behalf of my two best friends, Yasha Bugoenko and Semen Safronov, as well as myself (Semen was later killed in action and Yasha stayed in the academy the whole war). I was refused, the official statement saying I was needed at the academy to train pilots. I repeated my request a month later and was refused again: the front needed thousands of pilots and who would train them?

I knew the I-16 like the back of my hand so I started thinking what to do. I had to do something! So I simulated sickness during aerobatic exercises and they took me off I-16s and put me on UT-2s as a chief pilot. There were six squadrons scattered all over Middle Asia from Chimkent to Jambul and I flew around delivering packages and letters. I liked that job. I lived in barracks at Jambul with my cadets, although I had a separate room and there was plenty of food. In fact, I'm still amazed that – whether advancing or retreating – we were always well supplied with food, fuel and oil. Even at Smolensk in the autumn of 1943, with roads like rivers of mud, our supplies arrived on time.

Soon a request came and I was sent to the Kharkov Air Force Academy, which had relocated to Alma-Ata. There was no flight training: just theory, tactics, aerodynamics, navigation, weather studies and engine studies. Upon graduation from this academy I was commissioned as a junior lieutenant and in early 1943 we were sent by train to Air Force HQ in Moscow. That journey was a whole story in itself! We eventually made it to Moscow half-starved and from there I was sent on to the First Air Army, which was then based at Orel. From there I was sent to the 10th Bomber Regiment, which flew Pe-2s. I hardly made it out of there – I was a fighter pilot, after all! So they sent me back to the personnel section of the First Air Army.

When I arrived the place was packed. I was a junior lieutenant among crowds of majors and lieutenant colonels. They received five or six men a day and many officers had been waiting in line over two weeks. What could I do? The Commander of the air army was Mikhail Gromov.[2] So I invented the story that my sister was Gromov's wife! Striding into the personnel office I was stopped by an officer: 'Where are you going Lieutenant?' – 'I need to speak to the Chief of the Personnel Section.' – 'There are 300 officers in line here, many of them majors and lieutenant colonels, why are you trying to jump the queue, *Junior Lieutenant*?' – 'It's a private matter. I am Gromov's relative. My sister is his wife.' The officer immediately reported to Major Zhuk, Chief of the Personnel Section. Some ten minutes passed and I was called into the room. I walked in and introduced myself: 'Do you know the Army Commander?' – 'My sister is his wife, of course I know him.' – 'Are you a fighter pilot?' – 'Yes I am.' – 'Which planes did you fly?' I listed the types. 'Did you fly Yaks?' I lied: 'Yes I did.' – 'Here is the recommendation to the 303rd Fighter Division.' He wrote a letter for me to report to the 168th Regiment. The 303rd Division had three regiments of Yaks: 168th, 20th Guards and 18th Guards, while the 523rd flew Lavochkins. That's how I came to the 168th Regiment.

When I arrived at the regiment there were almost no pilots left – they'd all been killed. I was attached to the 1st Squadron and the Commander gathered us for a preliminary training session, saying: 'Tomorrow morning I'll check your skills.' Then he asked me: 'Did you fly Yaks?' – 'Yes, I was a flight instructor.' – 'Good, we need guys like you.' But I had the impression he didn't quite believe me. The session continued and the Commander asked some general questions on aerobatics and navigation. But suddenly he turned to me: 'How do you lower the landing gear on a Yak-1?' On the I-16 you had to roll a handle, but I'd heard that Yaks had some sort of tap that lowered the wheels automatically. And so I confidently answered: 'You have to open a tap.' – 'What tap?' Now I was in trouble! I thought to myself, 'How the hell should I know?' I hesitated and the Commander repeated, 'What tap?' – 'Well ... it looks like a water tap ...' The whole squadron rolled on the floor with laughter. The Squadron Commander told me: 'We have a two-seater training plane. I was planning to check your skills last but I've changed my mind and you will fly first.' I didn't know the control panel of the Yak. I thought: 'What should I do?' But I was lucky: the two-seater broke down. When the Squadron Commander dismissed the class I ran to the airfield and climbed into a Yak, which I'd only seen in the air before. I sat down, looked at the control panel, and compared it with the I-16. I called a technician, saying: 'Hey, I've forgotten a few things ...' He told me everything about the Yak. Next day I flew three circles with the Squadron Commander and then flew solo. That's how I started flying Yaks.

Soon many young pilots arrived. My Squadron Commander (I don't remember his name, but after him our squadron was commanded by Ilya I. Petrov[3]) told me: 'Can you test-fly them as first pilot?' I trained them for five days solid, getting plenty of flying practice myself in the process. Shortly afterwards I was promoted to lieutenant, becoming a senior pilot and then a flight commander. By the end of the war I was a captain and deputy squadron commander.

* * *

My first battle mission with the 168th Regiment involved escorting bombers in the Orel area. It's difficult to describe the situation in the air – there was a huge number of planes zooming about. I remember we were in a dogfight, but I just stayed behind my leader, so as not to lose him. Of course I had flying experience, but the first battle is always hard. For a start I had to learn to look around: you had to spot the enemy first if you wanted to survive. But this could be a tricky thing to do, especially when the enemy flew in small groups. Meanwhile clouds or glare from the sun might obscure your view; and when planes flew below you their silhouettes would be lost against the ground. If you didn't keep your eyes peeled you'd be sure to get a Messer or an FW 190 on your tail.

Dogfights were stressful. You could barely distinguish between friend and foe. Alex Batyuk even collided with an La-5 in battle. While we pilots of the 168th were in Yaks, those of the 523rd Regiment were in La-5s. As for the Germans, they had both FW 190s and Me 109s – quite a mixture! And what a merry-go-round: ascending aerobatics, fighting turns, flips – everyone was trying to get on everyone else's tail! I was always very wary of colliding with my colleagues: sometimes we flew a mere 5–10m from each other at high speed. Dogfights usually occurred in the vertical plane, which was just as well, because the Yak was strong in vertical flight. In comparison the I-16 had to fight on turns due to its lower speed: although its turn radius was 1.5 times smaller than that of a Messer.

In December 1943, in the Yelnya area of Smolensk, we six fighters escorted six Il-2s. Messers engaged us and a vertical merry-go-round began. I was ready to get an Me 109 in my sight when I saw that Ramenski, my wingman, was attacked by a Messer from behind. Although I had a perfect position for attack I left my Messer in order to help my wingman. The German saw I was going for a head-on attack and took the challenge. The altitude was 1,500m. I caught him in my sight and pulled the trigger. He fired simultaneously, his burst slicing off my left wing. My plane flipped upside down and fell, suddenly catching fire. I opened the canopy, and after some effort, managed to bail out. I pulled the ripcord, my parachute opened, and I landed in snow. A fire fight was going on nearby but no one was firing at me. My plane crashed somewhere. I heard a noise and suddenly one of our infantrymen grabbed me: 'Who are you?' – 'A senior lieutenant, a pilot ...' – 'My God! We saw you. Dogfights are an awful thing. How can you fly up there? We mistook you for the German – his plane crashed nearby.'

They took me to their Company Commander. I told him my story and the soldiers confirmed it. We downed a shot of pure alcohol, then the Commander gave me a horse and sled, plus an escort, which took me to a nearby village. Next day a car from the regiment picked me up.

*   *   *

The hardest plane to escort? Oh, *Shturmoviks*! Escorts would normally be set up like this: say there were six *Shturmoviks* and six fighters – a pair on the left, a pair on the right, and the third pair in rear at higher altitude. The *Shturmoviks* flew slowly, about 350km an hour. But if we fighters had flown at this speed we'd have been sitting ducks. That's why we normally flew above the group, either in circles or loops (like a figure of eight). I would often fly as wingman for the Regimental navigator, Grisha Titarev.[4] He would fly straight, while I flew below him, manoeuvring from left to right at higher speed. This made it easier for me to repel any attack on Titarev. Of course I was using more fuel but we didn't fly long-range missions. Nevertheless, you had to keep your eye on the fuel indicator especially in a Yak-3, for it only had enough juice for 50 minutes of flight. But in all other respects it was a great fighter.

The only planes that were harder to escort than *Shturmoviks* were those of our own top brass. We had a Chief of Air Arms Service, Major Kalashnikov, born in 1910. On the ground he pretended to be such a fighter – ready to shoot down all Fritzes! But it was very hard to fly with him. He flew as a wingman and stuck to me like glue at 50m so the other planes would cover him in case Messers attacked. Thank God he did not fly often! Our regimental commander, Kogrushev,[5] also flew rarely. Then there was a senior pilot in Alexei Duhanin's flight called Paul Vorobiev. He spoke like Chapaev:[6] 'I can lead a regiment. I can lead an air division. I can probably lead an air corps. I will need to study in order to lead an air army. But I will never be able to lead a squadron ...' But the squadron is the backbone of any Air Force unit! A squadron commander had to locate the target while keeping an eye on his wingmen and the escorted group. He also had to lead his pilots in dogfights and stick to the route during long flights. This was the most responsible job in a fighter unit.

First we flew Yak-1s, then Yak-7s, and in late 1944 our regiment was re-equipped with Yak-9Ls, which could carry 400kg of bombs inside the fuselage. But this plane was hard to fly and wasn't armoured: even though we were constantly ordered to bomb airfields defended by flak and fighters. Thus we envied *Shturmoviks*: same job but at least some armour around you! After we'd dropped our bombs we were supposed to take part in dogfights. Sometimes we still had bombs and came under fighter attack. What could you do? Ditch the bombs, close the bomb hatches, and engage! Once, while under attack from Focke-Wulfs, my bomb hatches refused to close so I had to fight them with them open.

I remember when we raided Heiligenbal Airfield, south of Königsberg [now Kaliningrad – Ed.]. I led a group of 12 fighters. The weather was good on our side of the front line, but once over the target clouds forced us to fly as low as 100m. I decided to fly over Frisches Haff bay and approach the airfield from the German side, but the clouds were even lower there. We flew as low as 50m but we had to complete the mission. We dropped our bombs from a horizontal flight path. There were plenty of German planes on the ground so it was impossible to miss (normally we dropped bombs in a shallow dive at 30 degrees). No one attacked us. We returned and reported a completed mission. Later our intelligence confirmed the raid had been successful, as several German planes were destroyed on the ground. But Slava Ivanov did not make it back from that flight. Apparently he was shot down by flak.

* * *

How did I like the Yak-9L? It was OK. Of course it wasn't a real fighter when it carried a bomb load. We had to fly carefully with bombs as they could detonate. And if you were hit by flak when carrying bombs you'd blow up. We'd take 400kg of bombs, both FAB high-explosive ones and PTAB anti-tank ones, depending on our target.

In East Prussia, in February–March 1945, I escorted Pe-2 bombers with six fighters. FW 190s attacked us at an altitude of about 2,500m. My wingman was Kolya Ramenski.[7] The FW 190s were about 300m higher than we were and attacked us with a dive. The German pilots fought bravely till the last day. We charged them head-on and the fun started. Ramenski was attacked by an FW 190 from behind, which scored a hit on his armoured glass, but the round didn't penetrate. Ramenski barely held on but didn't disengage. Meanwhile I started a dance with a Focke-Wulf. I was almost on his tail when he escaped by flipping upside down. We were as low as 500m. I needed to turn just 30 degrees to get on his tail and that would have been his end. At that altitude he flipped again and dived. I chased him down and he crashed into the sea. I levelled my plane and looked to see if the German pilot surfaced, but he didn't. Then Ramenski joined me and we flew back. He was killed shortly afterwards.

We were based near Jurgeitschen in East Prussia. I was supposed to lead the squadron into a battle but the weather was so bad we took off one by one. Ramenski took off after me, as he was my wingman. When I made the first turn I looked around but couldn't see him. Eyewitnesses on the ground later told me that Ramenski, in trying to catch up with me, made too sharp a turn: his plane fell into a spin and crashed.

* * *

How many sorties did we fly each day? It all depended on the weather: from three to five sorties a day. We had an orderly in the squadron, an old man (what do I mean 'an old man'? He was in his fifties! But for us 20-year-old boys he was an old man). One morning he woke us up early, about 4 or 5am. We went outside and the sky was completely obscured by clouds. We told the old man: 'Savateich, why did you wake us up? Can't you see the clouds? Wake us up only if you see stars.' Next time he woke us up with: 'Comrade pilots, wake up! There are stars in the sky!' We woke up and went outside. There were three stars in the sky, the rest were hidden by clouds: 'Savateich, please count them the next time. If you count more than twenty stars, then you can wake us up.' After this he woke us up with the words: 'Comrade pilots, wake up! There are 27 stars in the sky!'

The number of sorties also depended on your mission. If it was a deep reconnaissance mission you could only fly one sortie a day. It would take you 90 minutes for such a mission. In the Insterburg area I was forced to land at the Normandie-Nieman Regiment's[8] airfield. I was almost out of fuel. I flew over the airfield and saw planes in unfamiliar camouflage, so I thought they were German. I flew down to 50m and saw they were Yaks – but French ones. I landed and a technician ran up: 'What's wrong?' – 'I'm out of fuel.' French pilots walked up. At Smolensk we'd been based at the same airfield as them: playing football, drinking and partying together. They took heavy losses at the beginning, being too eager to engage the Germans. They chased them all over the place, leaving their escortees unprotected. Thus our pilots – and especially *Shturmoviks* – were not keen on having the French fighters as escorts. Anyway, they refuelled me and I flew back to my airfield.

Did we wear our decorations in combat? I did. Some pilots didn't wear them. One hot day we had to fly to a new airfield. A pilot put his tunic with all his decorations into the cockpit: when he was landing, and opened the canopy, the tunic was sucked out by the wind! It was quite a difficult task to get new decorations after the war – a kind of bureaucratic obstacle course. Kolya Apollonin came to our regiment in early March. I remember very well that he had the Gold Star of a 'Hero of the Soviet Union' on his breast. It seemed a bit strange to us that he sometimes took it off and sometimes put it on again. You say that he was not a 'Hero of the Soviet Union'?! Ah, now I see! We had suspicions back then, but he was older than us and we thought of him as a 'Hero of the Baltic sky', so we felt uncomfortable asking him about it.

* * *

The hardest plane to shoot down? It was harder to shoot down a fighter – bombers were less manoeuvrable. And the hardest fighter to shoot down was the FW 190. In comparison with a Messer it was faster, more manoeuvrable, and had better weapons. It had a radial air-cooled engine in front, which was almost like armour, and it was armoured from behind. We only engaged German bombers once. We four fighters attacked them when they were taking off from their airfield. It was a free-for-all!

A 'kill' was counted as a shared victory if the plane was shot down as a result of an attack by several pilots. For example, I attacked him first and then my wingman followed. But we didn't care so much about victories then. You would take off and think this flight was your last. That's why we didn't check our flight books – we felt like goners. I would only take a pistol and ammo with me so I could make it to the Partisans in case I was shot down. I had a look at our records after the war. They were complied in a very inaccurate manner, as pilots didn't check them. Many incidents were not recorded, others were written up incorrectly. The squadron's Liaison Officer was Frolov, a former pilot, and it was his job to take care of all paperwork. No one ever checked him. What did he write in the records? Did he exaggerate? We never did.

Were we superstitious? Many considered it unlucky to shave before a flight. I only shaved in the evenings after a day's work or in the morning if the weather was bad. I don't remember any talismans in the regiment.

Relations with technicians and mechanics were always very good. They worried about us and always waited for our return. Maintenance was excellent. I can still remember my mechanic, Sergeant-Major Sadovnikov. He was a very diligent worker. Once I came back from a mission with holes in the wings and my stabilizer damaged by flak. They managed to restore it overnight! The Squadron Engineer was Grisha Bogdanov, a hard-working guy. Relations with the Airfield Service Battalion were normally good, but sometimes there were fights with them.

* * *

I recall my last mission. It all goes back to early April 1945, when we were in Jurgeitschen at a large German airfield. My engine failed on the way back from a sortie. Turned out it had been damaged in a dogfight, but it worked till the airfield and only stopped at the first turn. I made it to the third turn and started to descend like a glider. I somehow made it between the metal columns of a destroyed hangar, landing without lowering the landing gear. The plane crashed on its belly, almost going nose over, and I sustained slight concussion. I was sitting there with no clue what had happened – I couldn't even get out of the cockpit. Then some mechanics drove up, pulled me out, and I ended up in hospital. After two weeks I was beginning to feel better, so I sent a letter to the regiment, asking them to send a U-2 plane to pick me up. But the doctor wouldn't let me go. He said I needed at least ten more days to recover. I decided to escape anyway. As requested, a U-2 plane from the regiment landed in a small field next to the hospital: I climbed in and flew back to the front.

Next day we flew to Insterburg Airfield at Königsberg. We stayed there overnight. It was so cold we had to hug each other to keep warm. In the morning we went for breakfast but I didn't feel well. I was troubled by a sense of foreboding: 'Today I will not return from this mission.' But I couldn't express my fears and tried to bury my black thoughts. Once in the air I felt comfortable. The situation was familiar and I had confidence in my skills. I thought they could no longer shoot me down. Petrov and I led two groups within a huge formation – our entire fighter division. I was flying a Yak-9L.

The bombers were to strike at Fischhausen Airfield on the Baltic coast. *Shturmoviks* strafed the target while we followed, dropping bombs in a shallow dive. We had no sights for bombing but dropped them as we pleased from low altitude – it was hard to miss. After dropping our bombs we joined the Pe-2s, in order to give cover. We climbed up to them alright but came under attack from several groups of FW 190s and Messers. A dogfight commenced and my wingman lost me. A German got on my tail. I tried to escape by flipping upside down but a second Fritz – apparently a Messer – was waiting: he opened fire and hit the centre of my wing, where the fuel tanks were situated. A fire started and flames soon spread to the cockpit. I made a battle turn, taking a bearing of 90 degrees. Suffocating, I opened the canopy: flames immediately enveloped me, forcing me to close it again. When I began inhaling flames instead of air I knew I had to bail out. It all took seconds – not minutes but seconds.

I didn't decrease throttle: I was hurtling into a descent. I opened the canopy a second time and was again assailed by flames. I unfastened my waist belt (we never fastened shoulder belts) and tried to crawl out. Putting my feet on the seat I pushed upward, struggling to get free, but fell back into the burning cockpit. A second attempt to bail out ended with the same result. Now the flames were licking my face. I thought the end had come. My whole life flashed before my eyes: where I was born, my school, my childhood friends with whom I went to steal water melons …

I gathered all my powers for a final effort, pushing my head and shoulders out of the cockpit. The incoming stream of air pressed me hard against the fuselage, but as the plane was in a chaotic downfall aerodynamic forces sucked me out, casting me clear of the plane.

Suddenly all was silent. Seconds later I heard an explosion as my plane hit the ground. I pulled the ripcord but the parachute didn't open at first. Then – with a feeling of great relief – I heard it flap open and I was left hanging. At that moment they opened fire from the ground, hitting me in the legs and neck. I pulled the ropes, miscalculated my speed, and hit the ground hard, losing consciousness.

When I awoke Germans were all around. Actually, to be more precise, they were Russians in German uniforms. They'd already taken away my papers and were trying to rip off my two Orders of the Red Banner. I was lying on the ground when a guy, probably an officer, came up: 'Are you from Belgorod?' What could I say? My lips were scorched and my face burned black as a pig-iron frying pan. He told his men: 'He's from Belgorod – his father was responsible for deporting *Kulaks*. Execute him!' They pulled me away for execution when an Opel drove up. Two German officers in leather coats got out. One of them yelled: 'As you were!' Then they pulled me into the car and took me to a CP for interrogation. That's how I ended up in captivity.

They took me to some HQ. I asked them to dress my wounds and a medic came and bandaged me all over, leaving just my mouth and eyes open. Then they started an interrogation. I lied as best I could, giving bogus information about my unit. After the interrogation they put me in a truck with three more Russian POWs. As I understood, they took us to Pillau. On the way – the journey took about an hour – I realized from the conversation that my comrades were an infantryman, a tanker and a scout. Aircraft roared over our truck. The Germans stopped, shoved us out, and stood us up against the wall of a stone barn. The guards – a driver and two soldiers – stepped back to the truck and struck up a conversation. I understood that they intended to execute us. At that moment *Shturmoviks* came flying in, spotting the truck and hitting it with RS missiles! The Germans were killed instantly, while we, falling on our knees and bellies near the wall of the barn, survived.

We lay low for a while but saw no more Germans. I offered to guide the other guys back to our lines, as I knew the area and could find my way, but no one followed me and I left alone. By nightfall I'd reached a strip of forest. My powers deserted me and I became feverish. I fell into a ditch and felt I was losing consciousness. At that moment I heard voices nearby. Some German soldiers grabbed me and shoved me into another truck. This time the vehicle was packed with POWs, many of them badly wounded. I assumed we would be executed and didn't even dream of surviving. When the truck stopped and the guards opened the door I saw the Baltic: it was the German Naval base at Pillau; music was playing and German officers were dancing ...

They marched us through the town. I automatically tried to remember the road we were taken by – I was a pilot, it was force of habit! They brought us to some building surrounded by a barbed-wire fence. There we were sorted into groups and I, as a pilot, was taken in. When I entered I saw a huge portrait of Hitler, stretching from ceiling to floor. My hands were bandaged so I couldn't pinch myself, but I touched the portrait anyway, just to make sure I wasn't dreaming.

They took me into another stone building. The door opened and I heard the buzz of voices. There were perhaps 100 or 200 POWs inside, mostly from the USSR. I tried to make myself comfortable on some hay, which had been scattered on the concrete floor, but two men in Russian uniform came up: 'Don't stay here, there are many traitors, come with us.' They took me to a corner and we introduced ourselves. One was called Kolya, he was a junior lieutenant, a tanker. The second was a scout, a senior sergeant, but I don't remember his name. I told them: 'My skin is burning, I can't see a thing. I need new bandages.' One of them dashed off and brought a nurse. The nurse was Russian, from the Yelnya area I think. When the Germans occupied Yelnya she dated German officers, leaving with them during their retreat. She made it as far as Pillau, where she enrolled as a nurse in the camp hospital. Sensing that the Red Army could not be stopped, and the end was near, she did her best to assist POWs. She brought me to a room where a German doctor was working with an assistant. The doctor spoke Russian quite well. As he took off the bandages – the pain was hellish – he told me: 'You'll probably survive, but you'll have scars on your face. You've been badly burned, you don't have a nose, and your mouth is scalded.' They washed me with potassium permanganate, bandaged me, and took me back into the POW building. Despite severe pain, I dozed off.

When I awoke I couldn't open my eyes, as the scorched eyelids had stuck together. I thought I'd lost my sight. The tanker, Kolya, again found the nurse. She washed my eyes with boric acid, repeating the procedure over the ten days. In addition she brought me chocolate to drink, which Kolya heated in a lamp made from an empty cartridge shell, as my burns made it impossible to eat.

The city was constantly bombed. During an air raid a bomb exploded next to our building and my legs were hit by debris from the falling roof. Somehow my two comrades managed to crawl out of the collapsed building but many were killed. The guys pulled me into a trench next to the destroyed building and we lived there some five more days. As the air raids were severe, and the fence around the camp destroyed, I urged the guys to escape. The Senior Sergeant told me that many tried to escape but were either betrayed or caught. Either way, all escapers were executed. But gradually I managed to talk them into it, especially since I had a plan to steal a rowing boat from the nearby harbour and row back to Soviet territory. We decided to escape during the night of 25–26 April.

But on the 24th we heard that the Germans were loading POWs onto barges and sending them God knew where. Some said the barges went to Sweden, others that they were sunk out at sea. We agreed not to leave each other, and to meet at our trench, just in case. At one in the morning we heard shouts: the Germans were rounding up more POWs for the barges, which were gathering in the harbour. Then they started sorting us by rank, forming several columns of POWs – literally hundreds and thousands of men. The moon was shining brightly and I could see everything. But the guards paid no attention to me – they thought I was a goner anyway – so I shuffled on a bit, then sat down. And so the POWs marched off with their guards while I stayed put. Now what should I do? Somehow I made it to a road where a German column was marching. I stopped but no German touched me: they could see I was completely covered with bandages and simply marched by. This huge column must have contained 1,000 men. Meanwhile planes filled the air: I couldn't tell if they were Russian or German. By a miracle I reached the road that led back to the bombed camp. Returning to our trench I found it empty. I hid there, eventually falling asleep.

The sound of approaching voices woke me: it was my two friends! They'd also escaped from the column. We spent the remainder of the night and all the following day in the trench. Then, under cover of darkness, the guys made their way to the shore in search of a boat. Having found a suitable craft and oars, they returned to collect me, and soon we were sailing east, finding our way by the stars.

We rowed until dawn, when I told the guys: 'Either the Russian or the German Air Force will execute us in daytime. I used to do it myself, firing at ships. We have to make it ashore, otherwise we're dead.' By 6am we'd almost made landfall, approaching a darkened coastline. I heard voices – Russian curses – and the next thing we were being hauled ashore. I was covered in bandages, my tunic hidden by a leather flight jacket, while the other guys were in German overcoats. A group of soldiers surrounded our boat: 'Damn Fritzes! You'll get it now!' We told them that we were Soviet POWs but they wouldn't listen: they saw the German coats and decided we were enemy scouts. My comrades pointed at me: 'He is a Soviet pilot, a captain.' The men pulled off my jacket and one shoulder board was still intact on my tunic. Next thing we were bundled off to their Battalion Commander. I don't know how they reported the incident to their *Kombat* but when we were escorted in someone said: 'Yes, they are German scouts, we should execute them.' I said: 'Wait, I'm a captain, a pilot, I'm badly wounded. *Kombat*, please ask them to change my bandages, I'm dying.' The *Kombat* ordered: 'Send this pilot to a hospital.' They put us on a small tank and we made our way, with some difficulty, through roads full of advancing troops.

I was taken to a surgery. Wounded men were stretched on tables and the air was full of groaning, curses and screams. Some 40 surgeons were at work. I was told to sit and wait. A table stood nearby. On it lay a huge Soviet soldier. They gave him vodka and he fell asleep, snoring loudly. Then they cut him open right before my eyes and extracted some splinters. The surgeon completed his work, prepared to cut open another guy, but suddenly turned to me: 'Captain, we have to tear off those bandages.' – 'Could you soak them first with potassium permanganate?' – 'Can't you see how many wounded we have here?' He began tearing off the bandages, which had stuck to my wounds, and the pain was indescribable. Unable to move, I endured this torment with screams of agony.

After my wounds were dressed with clean bandages I went outside to look for my two friends. I saw them in a truck full of liberated POWs. I made some sounds and caught their eyes. I waved my hand as the truck drove off. They left and I stayed: that's how we parted. I heard nothing of them after that. I was taken to hospital . . .

Kogrushev, the regimental commander, visited me on 1 May, accompanied by some other pilots. I was lying flat, almost unable to talk. They walked in, saw me, and froze with horror. They offered me a mirror but I refused. They brought some cognac. Kolya Kochmarik[9] said: 'Give us a needle, we'll pour some cognac in there.' I agreed and they put the needle between my lips and squirted out the cognac. I made two gulps and began to choke. As I coughed the skin on my face split and the blood began to pour. A surgeon came running: 'What the hell are you doing?!' It took me about two months to recover. My lips and nose peeled off some twenty times. I would literally take off the dead skin and throw it away. The pain was so bad that for the first 18–20 days I couldn't sleep unless injected with morphine.

In August I returned to my unit. I'd heard there was an order to send all former POWs for state investigation. My commander promised he would never send me, but in autumn 1945 a direct order came and there was nothing he could do. I had to go to the 12th Reserve Rifle Division, which was at Alkino station, near Ufa. I walked some 10km through the forest and finally approached the place: barbed-wire fence, guard towers, sentries with SMGs. I presented my papers and they let me in. There were crowds of men there – maybe 25,000 – all ex-Partisans and former POWs. There was a cavalry general, a friend of Marshal Budenny's, who kept repeating: 'I will write to Marshal Budenny, he'll get me out of here!' He was still in the camp when I left. After arrival I was interviewed by a detective from SMERSh, a senior lieutenant: 'Tell me how you ended up in German captivity.' I told him everything. I had my personal file with me. He looked through all the papers and said: 'Why did they send you here? You were in captivity only ten days and escaped. You have your personal file. I don't need you. You are free to go.'

That's how I went through inspection, but they didn't let me out, just transferred me to a barracks for those who'd been inspected. What did we do there? We'd get up in the morning, then take buckets to pick up breakfast. The food was awful, of course: lunch or dinner – it was just water. We played football and volleyball. And we had to play for a long time – till January. I would leave the camp with those who went for work and go to Alkino station. Then I'd take a train to Ufa for a couple of days, buy vodka, eggs, lard, eat enough for myself, and bring the rest back to my friends. I even went to dancing parties. The detective called me again ten days after that first interview. We spoke for 15 minutes and he told me: 'You are free to go. I don't need you here.' – 'How the hell do I get out of here?' – 'That does not depend on me.'

I met Boris Fedotov in the camp. He was a pilot from my regiment who was shot down over Orsha in 1943. He really helped me. When I was on my way to the camp, the Regimental Commander and the NKVD officer told me: 'You'll be back in a couple of weeks!' So I went there with only a tunic and jacket. But winter came with temperatures of minus 40. The barracks were not heated and the doors difficult to close. Boris was dressed in German clothes: padded trousers and warm overcoat. So we would sleep like this: he and his other friend from the camp would lie to my left and right, I would be in the middle, and we'd cover ourselves with two overcoats. In that way I slept for several months.

By the way, 'Hero of the Soviet Union' Senior Lieutenant Trud[10] was also held in that camp. He was Pokryshkin's wingman. As Trud told us, Pokryshkin would fly with six or eight fighters as a leader. In combat he'd say: 'I'm attacking, you all cover me!' He'd climb to 6,000m, while dogfights normally took place at 1,500–3,500m. He flew a P-39 Airacobra, which is a stable plane – like an iron – and has great speed, strong weapons, and a cockpit with a perfect view (I flew them after the war in the 72nd Guards Regiment). So five or six pilots were just covering him, making sure no one approached him. He'd dive at the enemy at immense speed, execute some pilot, and fly away. The group would repeat the manoeuvre after him. If a German group dispersed, they'd repeat the attack alone or in pairs.

I was released in January and in Moscow they sent me to the 72nd Guards Fighter Regiment. But the 'former POW' label stuck, making life difficult. In 1948 or 1949 I was working in an Air Force academy at Frunze, when an NKVD inspector came from Divisional HQ. Everyone was interrogated, including me. He interrogated me and then asked: 'Why didn't you shoot yourself?' I had to stop myself from shooting him on the spot. I told him: 'First of all I was wounded and my hands did not function, so I couldn't get my pistol out. Then they ripped off my pistol when I landed. They also ripped off my decorations.' What an asshole! To conclude, I flew 149 sorties during the war, took part in 39 dogfights, and scored nine individual and five shared victories.[11]

Notes

1. Valery Chkalov (1904–38) set several records for long-distance flight, becoming a popular hero in the USSR.

2. Lieutenant General Mikhail M. Gromov was a test pilot before the war, breaking several records for long-distance flight. During the Great Patriotic War he became Commander of the 1st and 3rd Air Armies of the Kalinin Front. A 'Hero of the Soviet Union', he received the Order of Lenin (5 times), the Order of the Red Banner (4 times), the Order of Suvorov 2nd Class, the Order of the Great Patriotic War 1st Class and the Order of the Red Star (three times).

3. Captain Ilya I. Petrov fought in the 168th Fighter Regiment. He flew about 200 sorties, scoring three individual victories. He was killed in a plane crash after the war.

4. Major Grigory I. Titarev fought in 168th Fighter Regiment. He flew about 200 sorties, scoring two individual victories.

5. Colonel Grigory A. Kogrushev was a veteran of the Spanish Civil War and the Great Patriotic War from the very first day, commanding the 11th and 162nd Fighter Regiments. He took command of the 168th Fighter Regiment from November 1943. He flew over 180 sorties during the war, scoring four individual and two shared victories. He received the Order of the Red Banner (twice), the Order of Alexander Nevski, the Order of the Great Patriotic War 1st Class, the Order of the Red Star.

6. Vasily I. Chapaev (1887–1919) was a hero of the Bolshevik Revolution, immortalized in books and films. Born a peasant, he rose to become a celebrated commander of the Russian Civil War.

7. Lieutenant Nikolai A. Ramenski fought in the 168th Fighter Regiment. He flew about 100 sorties, scoring three individual victories. He was killed in a plane crash in April 1945.

8. The Normandie-Nieman Squadron consisted of Free French pilots sent by General Charles de Gaulle to aid Soviet forces in 1943. The squadron flew Yak fighters and went on to become a highly decorated unit. The German High Command decreed that any captured French flyers would be executed.

9. Lieutenant Nikolai I. Kochmarik fought in the 168th Fighter Regiment. He flew about 100 sorties, scoring one individual victory.

10. Senior Lieutenant Andrei I. Trud fought in the 16th Guards Fighter Regiment. He flew over 600 sorties, scoring 24 individual and one shared victory. A 'Hero of the Soviet Union', he received the Order of Lenin, the Order of the Red Banner (three times),

the Order of the Great Patriotic War (twice), and the Order of the Red Star (twice).

11. Only one victory by A.F. Khaila is recorded in the archives of the units he fought with: on 8 April 1945, in the Rauschen area of East Prussia, he personally shot down an FW 190. Possibly his victories were scored over German-controlled territory and therefore not officially confirmed.

CHAPTER SIX

Ivan D. Gaidaenko

Interviewed by Artem Drabkin

Ivan Gaidaenko lives at his *dacha* near Moscow. After several attempts at giving me complicated directions we finally agreed to meet at a familiar crossroads. I followed his Ford *Ka* and arrived at the house, where we spent several hours chatting about planes and cars. We soon ran out of time, so I was obliged to arrange a second visit for the interview, which I did with pleasure.

I was born in Kirovograd, Ukraine. We lived in the suburbs, next to the airfield of an Air Force brigade. From my childhood I saw fighters and bombers flying. Once a plane crashed near our house: the pilot bailed out with a parachute and we little boys went running to see the wreck. Becoming a pilot was my childhood dream.

My father lost his life early and my family lived in poverty. After completing seven years of school I went to a machine-building college in order to gain a scholarship. In this way I hoped to get a decent job and so help support my mother.

We arranged a flying section at the city's *Osoaviakhim* and bought a glider with our own money. We launched it with a thick rubber band, like a huge bow. It flew well until one day a young girl crashed it.

With the slogan 'Our country needs 150,000 pilots!' a flying club was set up in Kirovograd. I was in the first batch of students to enrol. We were divided into three groups: pilots, pilot observers and technicians. I thought: 'A pilot is good but a pilot observer is even better!' And so I applied for the course. I didn't realize it was just another name for a navigator! Luckily they refused to take me: 'No, you were flying a glider, you should be a pilot.' And so I began my training. Over the course of a whole year we studied theory and practice in the evenings and at weekends. Meanwhile I had my college classes to attend! I remember we marched through the city in formation, wearing our flying overalls – it was so beautiful!

Upon graduating from flying club in 1937 (having studied the U-2) I was offered a place at the Odessa Air Force academy, named after Paulina Ossipenko.[1] The students consisted of two groups: those who had no flying training and guys like me from flying clubs. There were many students from the Caucasus (Georgians, Armenians, Azeri) and from the Ukraine. Those without flying experience were trained for two years: one year on U-2s and one on R-5s. But as a flying club graduate my course lasted less than a year, and we began flying R-5s immediately. I wanted to be a fighter pilot, but they don't ask you in the Army: if they told you to fly R-5s, you flew R-5s!

What can I say about the cadets at the academy? Most were uncultured guys from rural areas lacking a proper education. These shortcomings were fixed by our instructors and chaperones from the Odessa opera, which we visited at weekends – of course we visited other theatres too. Meanwhile our canteen tables seated four persons, as in a restaurant, and a brass orchestra would play. A sergeant-major would walk around and explain to cadets how they should hold their cutlery. These lessons in etiquette benefited many cadets later.

In 1938 I completed my 12 months' training. All young pilots were yearning for real action. We requested to be sent to the Far East, where battles with the Japanese at Khalkhin Gol had just ended. But the brass hats knew better and they sent me to Gatchina Airfield at Leningrad. The 333rd Detached Reconnaissance Squadron of R-5s was based there and we did a lot of training, flying day and night in bad weather conditions.

When the Winter War with Finland broke out in 1939 our squadron was sent to the north. We were based on Lake Kolajärvi, west of Kandalaksha. Our main tasks were reconnaissance and bombing raids. The Finns were fighting in small groups and we could only find them from their ski tracks in the forest. If we managed to catch them in the open, when they were crossing frozen lakes, we strafed and bombed them quite successfully. But we were lucky not to come across any Finnish planes: it was suicide to engage them in an R-5. What sort of armament did we have? A PV-1 machine gun at the front –

basically a Maxim fitted for airplanes – and two Degtyarev machine guns in rear. It was not a good war. Our leadership sucked. What could those infantry boys do in their ankle boots, leg wrappings, thin overcoats and *Budyonovka* hats? In fact two divisions froze to death.

Pilots from my squadron lived in a school building. We slept on bunk beds in the school's gym, while steam baths were arranged in a nearby tent. Well, we had to wash ourselves somehow! One day we went to the steam bath as they brought in a truckload of frozen dead. The corpses were contorted and twisted: so they were put in the steam bath, warmed up, and then straightened out. It was an awful sight. After this the corpses were buried with due ceremony.

We were also lucky the Finns had no AA artillery in our sector. They fired their small arms at us but without effect. Our squadron's only casualty came on the return flight to Gatchina, during a landing at Lodeinoe Pole. The squadron's Political Officer lost control of his plane – the landing gear was on skis, which made the craft unstable in a strong wind – and his propeller caught a pile of wooden bomb crates, breaking the tips. As the youngest in the squadron I was kicked out of my plane and the Political Officer flew it back to Gatchina. I was obliged to remain with the damaged craft, waiting for a new propeller to arrive. But fortunately I had a very experienced technician (in comparison with me, a teenager, he was an old man). He inspected the propeller, took a saw, made a few cuts to make the blades of equal length, and rounded them off. Then he launched the engine and we flew home without a hitch.

I received an Order of the Red Star for my part in the Winter War. It was handed to me personally by Mikhail I. Kalinin, President of the USSR. I was also entitled to free first-class rail tickets! What's more, we pilots were moved into a wing of Paul I's palace. Before the Winter War I'd been renting a corner in a private apartment block, my folding bed standing in a corridor. Now we had a single room for 18 pilots! I was considered the richest man in the dormitory. I had a gramophone, a rarity in those days, and a bicycle. Then I bought a watch. It was impossible to buy a watch! But with great difficulty I found and purchased a silver medallion watch. But I couldn't wear a medallion, so I gave it to a clockmaker and he converted it into a regular wrist watch.

How did we live in that room? The beds were arranged around a table, which stood in the middle. On this table my gramophone lived, surrounded by heaps of discs. In the evening we'd go out with girls, returning at midnight or later. Before going to sleep we'd set a disc playing, and when the next cadet came home he'd change it for another. By the way, we loved Klavdia Shulzhenko's songs the most.

We received excellent pay and our service uniform was beautiful, consisting of dark-blue tunic and trousers with high boots. Our flight uniform included fur-lined overalls, long felt boots and a leather coat. We were considered the military elite.

Right after the Winter War I attended a preparatory course for the Central Air Force Academy. Being a Ukrainian I had problems with the Russian language, and when I completed my first dictation I got an 'E' grade. Time passed. After the next dictation the teacher told me: 'Gaidaenko, you are making progress, now you have a "D"!' But when at Monino, where the Academy was (we were returning our R-5s in order to get new SBs), I saw the cadets being tortured with drill exercise. At that moment I decided not to go to the Academy after all – why should I put myself through such torment?

In the summer of 1940 we were relocated to Kexholm, which is now called Priozersk, and then to Pskov, where we took part in the establishment of Soviet power in Estonia. As we were told then: 'We are giving a brotherly helping hand to the friendly Estonian people.' What type of mission were we given? Say there was a column marching on the road: a commander's Emka car followed by trucks, tanks and infantry. We had to find that column, determine its position, and drop information regarding the line of advance. Then we had to wait for the column's written reply and pick it up. How was this done? We did it like this: between two poles a rope was set (not fastened to the poles but left loose). The written message was secured to the middle of this rope. Our task was to fly low, let down a hook, catch the rope, and pull the message into the cockpit. Such were communication systems in those days!

I can only speak of things I saw with my own eyes. As I flew over towns and villages I saw crowds of people welcoming our troops with red flags. No one could have forced the Estonians to welcome us like that, as they are saying now: for a start, there'd been no Soviet troops in those areas before! Although they now claim we came as occupiers, the establishment of bases was agreed with the Estonian government. In addition to this, our units were ordered to avoid conflicts with the local population at any cost.

In August we returned to Kexholm and received new SB planes. The squadron was merged with two others to form a reconnaissance regiment, which relocated to Siverskaya at Leningrad, as the airfield at Kexholm was too small for SBs.

Timoshenko's notorious Order No. 0362 was announced in December 1940. I, a lieutenant and squadron commander with an Order of the Red Star, was sent to live in barracks! And just to add to my misery I was appointed the billet's senior officer. I saw a lot of misery there, as you can imagine: for all those graduates from the academies – lieutenants, pilots and navigators – were suddenly demoted to NCOs. It was bad enough being squeezed into barracks, but to be demoted? It was a humiliation before sweethearts, friends and family! Of course, discipline suffered, and it was hard for me to keep my gang of disgruntled young pilots under control. Many of them went AWOL to drown their sorrows in drink. And when they ran out of money for booze they sold the linen from the dormitory. It was a total mess! Even *Komsomol* members got into trouble. One of them was summoned to a disciplinary hearing: 'Why are you drinking and making trouble? We will expel you from *Komsomol*!' – 'I don't care!' he replied, 'expel me! I'll be a Communist in my heart!' The outbreak of war helped: otherwise they'd have sentenced me for stealing state property!

*   *   *

War was in the air – we could sense it. But training still went on. On 21 June 1941 I got leave. I decided to visit a girl I knew in Kexholm before going home to the Ukraine. While I was packing the alarm sounded. We assumed it was a training alarm and ran to our white SB planes (they looked like swans to us), warmed up the engines and prepared for take off. We prepared photo cameras and attached dummy concrete bombs just in case. No one realized it was a real alarm! As late as 9 or 10 in the morning they announced the outbreak of hostilities. We removed those dummy bombs right away and replaced them with real ones. But instead of flying bombing raids we were ordered to repaint our planes in camouflage colours, and this took a couple of days. That's how my war began.

Siverskaya air base was not disturbed during the first days of the war. We flew a couple of scouting sorties over the Gulf of Finland and then our squadron was relocated north, to Afrikanda air base. The bomber regiment of the 1st Air Division was there. The division also had 145th and 147th Fighter Regiments. But the airfield had no air defences and suffered enemy strikes every day, Ju 88s bombing at will. Too many of our planes were knocked out on the ground, that's why we were sent there. What kind of leadership was this? They had two fighter regiments at hand while the bomber regiment was sitting there without air cover!

About a dozen MiG-3s were brought by rail. They asked for volunteers to retrain as fighter pilots so I stepped forward. They sent us Squadron Commander Novozhilov from the 145th Regiment with a UTI-4 to train us on. This plane was hard to fly after an SB. As a result, Novozhilov only let two pilots fly independently: me and another guy. The rest gave up because the I-16 and UTI-4 were both very demanding planes (in an SB you had to pull the stick with both hands, while on an I-16 you just had to touch it for the plane to start spinning). That's how I became a fighter pilot with the 145th Regiment. I didn't get to fly a MiG-3 though – they'd all been destroyed on the ground. They gave me an old I-16 with a finger-thick layer of paint on it. This plane was armed with two ShKAS machine guns: but they couldn't fire more than two bursts without jamming from overheating. Then they sent my group of five pilots to Alakurtti, where we flew scouting and ground assault missions.

I remember one sortie. A heavy KV tank got stuck in a swamp and was abandoned, although its crew should have blown it up. Can you imagine? We were ordered to destroy this tank with 7.62mm ShKAS machine guns! They should have known better! Well, we flew to the tank and fired at it. But what was the point of all this?

I engaged the enemy only once in an I-16. We were a group of three or four planes and we came across a Fiesler 'Storch'. We chased him all over the place but couldn't hit him! One of my machine guns jammed but eventually we succeeded in shooting him down.

The Germans soon reached the small river at the edge of our airfield, but they kept to their side of the river and we remained on ours. We couldn't quit because the fog was too thick for flying. Thank God the Germans didn't continue their advance! The Airfield Service Battalion had left, leaving us a little bread and some canned sprats. We soon ate the bread and were forced to live for three days on canned fish. To this day I can't stomach those sprats! But the weather began to clear on the third day, so we started the engines, took off without a proper warm-up, and rushed across the river to Afrikanda. Almost immediately after, in late September, we were sent to Seima Airfield at Gorki for retraining. There we received new LaGG-3s.

How did the retraining take place? There was a huge parking area at Seima stuffed with planes straight from factories. They counted the planes we needed and said: 'Test fly them and get out of here!' There were no training versions of the LaGG so we just had to get on with it, making a couple of flights around the airfield. But we had to work quickly, as there were many other regiments in the area, all waiting to get airborne. The LaGG was much more complicated than the I-16. The latter had only a stick and throttle, as well as a controlling device for the radiator cover. But the LaGG had controllable propeller pitch plus automatic retraction and protraction of the landing gear. Anyway, we learnt to fly it.

* * *

It was in December 1941 – with 40 degrees of frost – that we five crews from Kutakhov's 3rd Squadron were rushed forward to Obozerski, while the rest of the regiment remained behind Ivanovo. It was at Obozerski that we heard news of the counter-offensive at Moscow. We were so happy! After so many months of retreating our troops were now pushing forward. We pestered our top brass, asking to be sent to the front (why should we just sit around?) and we were ordered to Belomorsk. They sent us a Pe-2, which was supposed to be our lead plane. The navigator on the *Peshka* turned out to be a lieutenant I'd known from Kirovograd – I'd been a guest at his wedding. As we prepared to fly we noticed heavy clouds but took off with the *Peshka* leading. As we flew the clouds dropped lower and lower, enveloping the *Peshka*. But we took care to remain underneath, hugging the ground, and taking the railway line as our guide. Meanwhile the mist closed in, forcing us so low we almost scratched the tree tops. It was a difficult flight but eventually we landed at Belomorsk. But where was the *Peshka*? It turned out the Lieutenant got lost in the clouds and crashed: apparently he didn't know how to fly in foul weather.

While waiting for our regiment to arrive we were attached to the 609th Fighter Regiment under Leonid Galchenko (he'd been Squadron Commander in our 145th Regiment and was later appointed a regimental commander). We were deployed against Finns in the Segezha area, south of Belomorsk. Once we ran into Brewsters – the Finns had such planes – and shot down a couple. When we engaged them they climbed into the clouds and I followed. As I made my way through the mist I saw one of our LaGGs firing one burst after another – but at what? I could see no target! I flew closer and saw Galchenko's symbol – a black cat – on the tail. But that day we were short of aircraft and Viktor Mironov, Galchenko's favourite, was flying his plane. Mironov noticed me and pulled away, disappearing into the clouds. When we landed the inquiry began into who had scored what. Mironov claimed he'd scored a victory: 'Look how much ammo I used – more than everyone else!' I replied: 'You asshole, you just wasted your ammo above the clouds. I saw you firing into thin air!' We had such a quarrel that I ended by saying: 'I'll never fight in this regiment again!' By this time my regiment had already arrived but Galchenko wouldn't let me go, saying: 'You'll fight the war in this regiment!' Next time we flew a sortie there was no dogfight, so when the other guys started landing I turned round and flew back to my own regiment. When I landed my Regimental Commander said: 'Great job, those guys can go to hell!'

Many officers left the 145th (later the 19th Guards Regiment) to command other regiments. For example, Vladimir S. Mironenko was commissioned as commander of the 195th Regiment in 1943. Before his new posting he was Squadron Commander and I was his deputy. Vladimir lost his life in a stupid way. He liked drinking but alcoholism is an awful thing. He gathered his pilots and told them: 'You damn idiots can't fly, you'll all get shot down! Now watch me, this is the way to do it!' Mironenko took off and started performing aerobatics at low altitude – then crashed. By the way, Mironov also died in an accident. He was given an La-5 – a brand-new plane at the time – and came flying to our airfield at Shongui to show off his aerobatics. I wasn't there but I heard from the other guys that he crashed. We had a lot of such losses.

I fought on LaGG-3s from late 1941, but in 1942 ours was the first regiment in the USSR to get Airacobras.[2] The first Cobras came from England. The English shipped their planes differently to us. We always washed them, while their Cobras came to us dirty. They were brought by ships and delivered to Afrikanda. But the main problem was they arrived without manuals. For a long time we couldn't work out how the brakes functioned: our planes had pneumatic brakes controlled by a handle; these had hydraulic brakes, like those of a bomber, controlled by a pedal.

The Cobra had another feature: its landing gear was different to ours. Russian fighters had a rear wheel, so in order to take off one had to pull the stick, gain speed on the ground, lift the tail, gain more speed, then pull the stick again. But the Cobra's third wheel was in front so there was no need to lift the tail. Without a manual, however, no one guessed this. Well, Kutakhov was the first to test fly a Cobra. Having started the engine he pulled the stick and the plane shot across the airfield. Eventually he managed to take off, but only later did we realize the stick had to be kept in neutral, allowing the front wheel to take off, followed by the whole plane. But when we finally mastered the Cobra we fought very well. That was in 1942, the hardest year of all. The Germans were going for Murmansk and we were defending the city from the sky. At first the Germans used old models of Me 109s and 110s. The Cobra was superior and we beat them up good. Cobras were light and armed with a 20mm gun, two large-calibre machine guns and four machine guns of rifle calibre in the wings. I removed the wing machine guns from my Cobra and it was a perfect plane, even in vertical fights. The Germans were no match for us! But this easy life ended when they received modern 109s: then they started chasing us around again.

Our regiment was moved back and forth between Belomorsk in the south and Murmansk in the north. Typically our missions involved covering Murmansk, the railway, and our ground troops. But sometimes we escorted ground assault planes: a regiment of *Shturmoviks* – later it became the 17th Guards Regiment – being attached to us for a while. Their pilots were trained worse than our young replacements! They were particularly bad at navigation so we had to provide a pilot to lead them. Our pilot would locate the target, dive towards it, and the *Shturmoviks* would follow. A crazy incident took place once. We escorted those Il-2s on a mission and one of our guys flew in front as a guide. The weather was atrocious – snowstorms – so we couldn't make it to the front line. After flying around for some time we arrived at Murmansk, which had an AA gun on every hill and on every ship. When Allied convoys arrived in Murmansk the port was completely packed with ships and any bomb would have found a target: consequently, no one was allowed to fly there, as the flak batteries opened up on all aircraft without waiting to identify them. Thus we found ourselves in the thick of an AA barrage! Nevertheless, we managed to lead the *Shturmoviks* away safely, heading for their base at Murmashi, where our lead fighter made a shallow dive and then climbed away. But the *Shturmovik* boys had been so shaken by the flak that they bombed their own airfield before landing on it! Such was their level of training.

*　*　*

I was shot down on 16 May 1942. It happened like this. Eight fighters under Kutakhov were scrambled for air cover over Murmansk. Kutakhov – or 'Father' as we called him – led the group while I flew in rear. They usually put me or Bochkov at the back because we had perfect eyesight (they used to say to me: 'The Germans are just taking off and you are already counting them!'). Well, we intercepted a group of Germans: about 12 Ju 88s and the same number of fighters. The Fritzes immediately turned away and we followed without attacking. Then they doubled back, but we weren't going to let them reach Murmansk, so they made another loop and again we followed. This manoeuvre was repeated two or three times. Eventually we radioed to Kutakhov: 'Father, come on, what are you waiting for? Attack!' We were impatient for battle, even though outnumbered: the Germans would have never attacked in such a situation! And so Kutakhov attacked and was the first to get shot down. But he managed to bail out and I saw his gangling figure dangling from a parachute. Naturally I was worried. The German pilots were assholes – those who say they were like chivalrous knights are mistaken – they'd finish off parachutists with a few extra bursts. And sure enough, as Kutakhov descended, the Germans began firing at him. I tried to prevent this by circling round Kutakhov: a moment later a round struck me, apparently penetrating the oil tank.

But the engagement was over and we headed home at low altitude. It was only then that I caught the acrid smell of smoke and noticed my oil was leaking away. Next thing the engine jammed and began to burn. What could I do? I was flying too low to bail out. But I was sitting in a ticking time bomb! My plane was on fire and I knew I had to get out as soon as possible. Fortunately there was still a lot of snow on the ground and spotting a small valley, I decided to crash land. I secured my safety belts as best I could, pressed my hand against the control panel, and prepared to hit the ground. I don't remember any more. When I regained my senses I was about 10m from the plane, which was smoking but not actually burning. I must have unfastened my belts and crawled from the wreck while unconscious . . .

*　*　*

The strengths and weaknesses of the Cobra? First of all, I must say that I loved this plane. It was only on Cobras that I fought with confidence in dogfights. Although I scored a victory on an LaGG-3 (a better fighter than the I-16) the Cobra was superior: the cockpit, visibility, radio and steering were all excellent.

The Cobra had good sights so there was no need to 'fire when you see the rivets,' as we used to say. Although pilots would aim by firing bursts of tracers from large-calibre machine guns, I felt this unnecessary. Why? Because surprise is the most important thing in battle. But some of our pilots were too eager to fire: they'd bang out a burst of tracer and the enemy, forewarned of an attack, would immediately escape. But if there were no tracer bullets in the belt you could simply approach and kill. If you missed, you could come closer. That's how I saw it, and I asked ground crews not to load tracer rounds into my machine guns: but my requests were rarely heard.

The Cobra's cockpit was much better than the LaGG-3: all-round observation was very good. But the main thing was it had an excellent radio (for its time). It even had a radio semi-compass. When we received LaGG-3s, not all of them had radios. For example, wingmen would get receivers, while leaders would get both receivers and transmitters. What did this mean in battle? Say I was a wingman and spotted the enemy: without a transmitter how could I tell my comrades? But when we flew I-16s there was no radio at all! How were we supposed to cooperate or be guided to targets? Sometimes they'd tell us: 'Fly to area such-and-such and search for the enemy there.' In 1942, though, when we received Cobras, ground guiding was already set up, but there was a lack of radar.

Cobras also came with good dry tack: a separate package for every meal and everything was insulated. It had a good first-aid kit, too. It had a special syringe containing pain-killer. You just had to take off the cap and you could make the injection immediately. And the bandages were perfect. The problem was that you could only use all this stuff if you landed with your plane! As this was a rather unlikely scenario, pilots would take three or four chocolate bars and stuff them into their pockets or tape them to their parachutes. We'd also take a pistol and a couple of ammo clips. We didn't take the signal pistol. In addition to a TT pistol I also had a small German Mauser with me. Luckily I never had to fire my pistol at the enemy, but we fired at dummy targets on the ground. We had plenty of ammo.

1. Ivan D. Gaidaenko.

2. Nikolai G. Golodnikov.

3. Alexander F. Khaila.

4. Vitaly I. Klimenko.

5. Vitaly V. Rybalko.

6. Alexander E. Shvarev.

7. Viktor M. Sinaisky.

8. Members of a flying club. The second person on the left with a paratrooper badge is Nikolai E. Bespalov.

9. Cadets Ivan Shumaev and Vitaly Klimenko (on the right) of Chuguevo Air Academy studying theory of flying on the airfield at Kochetovka.

10. Polikarpov U-2 training plane. All future Soviet pilots of the 1930s trained on this biplane before switching to newer and faster planes. Cadet Yuri Afanasiev is in the rear cockpit.

11. Vitaly Klimenko in the academy's classroom in front of a stand displaying the M-11 engine.

12. and 13. *left and below:* Graduation photos.

14. *below:* Last serial model I-16 Type 29. Factory No. 21 produced 650 such planes. This 'Donkey' had an M-63 engine. The plane was armed with three synchronized machine guns: two ShKAS 7.62mm and one BS 12.7mm.

15. *below:* Vitaly Rybalko from the 122nd Fighter Regiment is in the cockpit of this MiG-3 named 'For the Motherland'. The high-altitude AM-35A engine made the plane fly at 640km per hour at an altitude of 7,800 metres, but at low altitudes, as pilots commented, it was as cumbersome as an 'iron'.

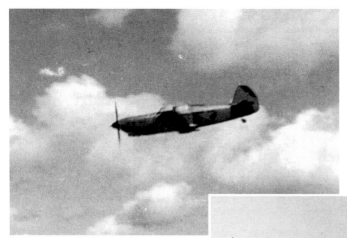

16. Yak-1 in flight. It was considered the best plane out of a triad of new fighters (LaGG-3, MiG-3 and Yak-1) that entered service before the war.

17. LaGG-3 in the air in winter 1941. Some pilots commented that LaGG stood for 'Lacquered Guaranteed Grave'! The heavy fuselage made from plywood and birch was later compensated by installation of the new ASh-82 engine, which turned this Cinderella into a princess La-5.

18. Repair of I-16 fighters at a Moscow plant.

19. As a result of these strikes and heavy air battles in the first two weeks of the war, most of the Soviet Air Force's planes in the Western Military Districts were lost.

20. Commander of 13th Fighter Regiment of the Baltic Fleet, 'Hero of the Soviet Union' I.G. Romanenko and mechanics near an I-16 fighter. Most likely the picture was taken in September 1941.

21. Soviet airfields were one of the Luftwaffe's priorities on 22 June 1941.

22. Mechanics prepare an I-16 for flight.

23. MiG-3 squadron over Moscow.

24. Fighters of the 156th Fighter Regiment waiting for a battle mission.

25. Commander of the 65th Ground Assault Regiment swears an oath as he receives the Guards Banner, transforming his unit into the 17th Guards. The regiment was equipped with Hurricanes at the time and many of the pilots standing in the formation were soon to fight in the 767th Fighter Regiment.

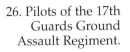

26. Pilots of the 17th Guards Ground Assault Regiment.

27. Repair of the I-16 and Il-2 in repair workshops.

28. Moscow air defence pilots with an I-16.

29. Breakfast in between sorties.

30. Loading a fighter's synchronized machine guns.

31. Dogfight over Murmansk in 1942.

32. Pilots on duty. A P-40E Kittyhawk fighter is in the background.

33. A sailor guards a captured German pilot (Murmansk 1942).

34. Wreckage of a downed German Me 110.

35. Vitaly Klimenko taking off from Sukromlya airfield to reconnoitre Olenino railway station (summer 1942).

36. Yak-1s from the 1st Guards Fighter Regiment taking off (summer 1942).

37. Pilots of the 1st Guards Fighter Regiment after a successful mission. From right to left: I. Tihonov, V. Klimenko, I. Zabegailo, Liaison Officer of the 1st Squadron Nikitin, and mechanics of the squadron.

38. V. Klimenko (sitting) and engineer of the 1st Guards Fighter Regiment inspecting the battle damage received by Klimenko's plane in a dogfight over Rzhev.

39. V. Klimenko joins the Communist Party in the cockpit of a U-2 before being sent to hospital (Sukromlya airfield, August 1942).

40. Political Officer of the 1st Squadron, 1st Guards Fighter Regiment, Kuznetsov (on the extreme right) congratulating pilots on a successful mission. From left to right: I. Zabegailo, V. Klimenko, I. Tihonov. The picture was taken on Sukromlya airfield at I. Zabegailo's plane.

41. V. Klimenko in the cockpit of a Yak-7B 'Trade Union worker'.

42. Alexander Shvarev (on the left) at his La-5FN.

43. Aces of the 40th Guards. From left to right: Ivan Semenyuk, Nikolai Kitaev, and Konstantin Novikov. The total victory tally of these three pilots numbered 72 individual and 24 shared victories.

44. Cadet N.G. Golodnikov of Eisk Naval Pilot Academy. The photo is from the cadet's personal file, dated 1940.

45. N.G. Golodnikov and Airacobra (Severomorsk airfield 1943).

46. Boris Safonov and British pilots from the 151st RAF Wing, which fought in the Soviet far north. A Hurricane fighter is in the background.

47. Pilots of the 2nd Guards Fighter Regiment of the North Fleet Air Force. A group photograph including Senior Lieutenant, Senior Pilot Yevgeny Gredyushko, Captain Viktor Maksimovich, Pilot Lieutenant Grigory Vorontsov.

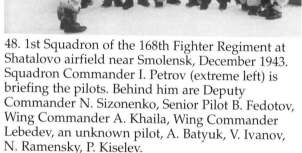

48. 1st Squadron of the 168th Fighter Regiment at Shatalovo airfield near Smolensk, December 1943. Squadron Commander I. Petrov (extreme left) is briefing the pilots. Behind him are Deputy Commander N. Sizonenko, Senior Pilot B. Fedotov, Wing Commander A. Khaila, Wing Commander Lebedev, an unknown pilot, A. Batyuk, V. Ivanov, N. Ramensky, P. Kiselev.

49. Commander of the 1st Squadron, 168th Fighter Regiment, I.I. Petrov (20 August 1945).

50. Pilots of the 168th Fighter Regiment near a Yak-9. From left to right: Nikolai Galetski, Ivan Khalchenko, Alexander 'Pan' Ivanovski.

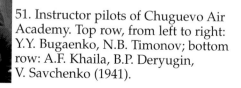

51. Instructor pilots of Chuguevo Air Academy. Top row, from left to right: Y.Y. Bugaenko, N.B. Timonov; bottom row: A.F. Khaila, B.P. Deryugin, V. Savchenko (1941).

52. 'Malyi Theatre for the Front' - the first of two Yak-9L squadrons to serve with the 168th Fighter Regiment. From the start of the war Soviet citizens and organizations were encouraged to give money for planes and tanks. In this case the Malyi Theatre raised 1 million *roubles* and 'bought' a squadron of Yaks.

53. A squadron of the 122nd Fighter Regiment. From left to right: Pilots Yarko, L. Andreev, V. Rybalko, M. Pugel, I. Kuskov, Yaroshenko. A Yak-9 is in the background (1944).

НЕ ЧИСЛОМ, А УМЕНИЕМ

Истребители Рыбалко сбили пять самолетов врага

Взвилась ракета. Один за другим поднялись в воздух четыре истребителя и пристроились к подошедшим штурмовикам.

Вскоре мы были уже над целью. В это время нашу четверку атаковали фашистские истребители. Капитан Овечкин и старший лейтенант Рыбалко, отражая нападение, в первой же схватке сбили по одному «Мессершмитту».

Штурмовики делали второй заход, когда из облаков

выскочили три пары фашистов. Немцы пытались атаковать «Ильюшиных». На перерез фашистам бросились лейтенант Пождаев и младший лейтенант Усков. Лейтенант Пождаев зашел одному «Мессершмитту» слева и ударом по фюзеляжу сразил его. Усков на правом боевом развороте с дистанции 70— 50 метров сбил второго «Мессершмитта».

Продолжая бой с остальными немецкими истребите-

лями, старший лейтенант Рыбалко атакой снизу в лоб зажег «МЕ-109». Фашист перевернулся и резким пикарованием пошел к земле.

Таким образом, четверка отважных советских летчиков под командой старшего лейтенанта Рыбалко, храбро защищая штурмовиков, в первом бою завоевала блестящую победу, сбив пять фашистских истребителей и не потеряв ни одного своего.

(От наш. корр.)

54. Fragment of a newspaper article recounting a battle by V. Rybalko's squadron.

55. 19th GIAP Regimental Commander Georgy I. Reifschneider poses near a newly arrived Airacobra (1942).

56. Lieutenant Colonel Ivan D. Gaidaenko (1947).

57. Ivan D. Gaidaenko in the cockpit of his Airacobra. The inscription can be translated as 'My pretty baby'.

58. La-5FN of the Navigator of the 40th Guards Fighter Regiment, Major A. Shvarev (autumn 1944).

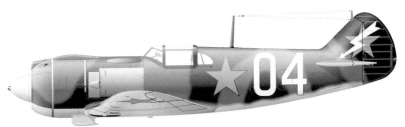

59. La-5 of the 98th Guards Fighter Regiment (Kursk, July 1943).

60. P-40A Kittyhawk of the 2nd Guards Fighter Regiment (spring-summer 1942).

61. MiG-3 of the 122nd Fighter Regiment as flown by Lieutenant V. Rybalko (spring-summer 1942).

62. Yak-9L of the 168th Fighter Regiment, as flown by Captain A. Khaila (spring 1945).

63. Hurricane of the 1st Guards Fighter Regiment (spring 1942).

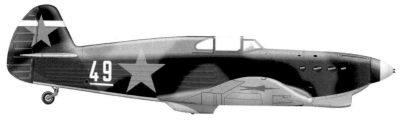

64. Yak-1 of Lieutenant V. Klimenko, 1st Guards Fighter Regiment (August 1942).

65. Yak-7B of the 1st Guards Fighter Regiment. The plane was lost during Operation Spark (breaking the Siege of Leningrad) in January 1943.

66. Air Force lieutenant in flight uniform (1935-41). The Lieutenant is dressed in flying jacket with collar tabs insignia, officer's webbing, flight webbing and a parachute. *(Photos courtesy of uniform collector Vadim Voskoboinikov.)*

67. Air Force lieutenant in field uniform (1940-41). The Lieutenant is dressed in a dark-blue side cap, summer khaki tunic with sleeve insignia model 1940 and pilot sleeve badge on the left shoulder, dark-blue trousers, officer's webbing and long boots.

68. Sleeve badge of Air Force pilots (the 'Chicken' mentioned in the text). According to an order of the People's Commissar of Defence, dated 17 December 1936, the sleeve badge was for middle-level and junior commanders (pilots, flight observers, navigators, flight bombardiers, flight radio-operators/gunners, flight engine operators/gunners). The badge was made obsolete by Order No. 25 of the People's Commissar of Defence, dated 15 January 1943.

The Cobra had weaknesses, however. For example the tail could bend under certain G-forces, so we had to strengthen them with metal bars. Meanwhile the Cobra's engine was not strong enough to engage a Messer in vertical flight. In fact, Cobra engines were quite sensitive and required good grease and good care. They contained silver-covered bearings: when these were new everything worked OK; but after servicing in a Russian repair shop engines frequently failed. God knows what kind of bearings they installed there! Luckily I didn't have engine failures myself.

Supercharging was also a problem. In Russian fighters I'd give full throttle and still be able to push the engine: but if I tried this in a Cobra over-supercharging would take place, fuel would detonate, and the engine would stall. That's why you had to be careful flying a Cobra and watch the supercharging all the time.

Another Cobra weakness was its 20mm cannon, which was worse than a Russian ShVAK. The latter had higher rate of fire – a very important feature. That said, I preferred foreign 20mm guns to the 37mm calibres. The latter fired so slow: bang ... bang ... bang! If I calculated the aiming point and fired, one round would fly above the target and the next – which was supposed to hit – would fly below. Of course, if you managed to hit an enemy with a 37mm round he was a goner, but achieving this feat was almost impossible. There was also very limited ammo storage with 37mm guns.

Finally, there was much talk about how easily Cobras fell into a spin. We had a pilot called Kuptsov in our regiment. Once, when flying above the airfield, he fell into a spin. I was on the ground observing his exercise and ordered him: 'Push the stick, get out of the spin!' Then I saw that his plane was too low and shouted: 'Bail out! Bail out!' But he didn't. The plane disappeared behind a forest and we saw a pillar of smoke – that was it. Kuptsov came down in the Kola peninsula, a northern wilderness with no villages, no nothing. There was only a railway with a few settlements along it. We couldn't make it to the crash site quickly, being obliged to fly over on U-2s. We found Kuptsov's plane sunk deep in boggy terrain. We dug like crazy but couldn't tell if the pilot was still inside or not. But as we saw no parachute we concluded he must have died in the crash. We waited a couple of days, but when Kuptsov didn't show up we arranged a 'funeral'. In such cases we'd make a coffin, put some artefacts or personal belongings inside, and bury it. And so our group solemnly marched to the cemetery. Suddenly a wild and dishevelled man emerged from the forest. He approached the burial party: 'Whose funeral is this?' – 'A pilot named Kuptsov died in a crash.' – 'But I'm still alive!' It turned out that Kuptsov bailed out at low altitude, his parachute opened, but he hit the ground hard. After recovering somewhat he gathered up his parachute and wandered around till he found the railway track, then he headed back to the airfield through the forest. Naturally everyone laughed at me for this: 'Tell us how you buried Kuptsov!'

If we compare the planes we produced during the war with the Lend-Lease ones, ours were better. For example, the war in the north was over in 1944 and many units were sent to the Far East. My regiment remained in the north, however, equipped with Kittyhawks. But I found out there were Yak-7Bs in Vologda, the regiment that normally flew them having gone East and left them behind. And so I made a deal and went over to pick up 12 Yak-7Bs (somehow, Kutakhov managed to get his hands on a Yak-3). As the war was over for us in the north, we decided to arrange training and exercise dog-fights: Kutakhov flew his Yak-3, I flew a Yak-7B, while Novozhilov and another regimental commander flew Cobras. During those dogfights we Yak pilots beat the Cobras very easily! In fact, I think the best wartime plane was the Yak – especially the Yak-3. It was so manoeuvrable that – with an experienced pilot at the controls – it was impossible to shoot down. The Yak-7B was also a formidable fighter.

*   *   *

Did we meet English and American pilots? We met the English pilots, although they'd been attached to the 2nd Guards Fighter Regiment of the Northern Fleet. One day we made it to Murmansk and met them, throwing a grand party. It was hard to find vodka so we drank after-shave lotion. If you added water it made a white liquid, which we dubbed 'white handkerchief'. We all got very drunk. So we had good relations. What would pilots quarrel about?

What did we do during our spare time? We'd sit around telling stories. Those who liked to drink just drank – an example being one of our pilots, Peter Aksentievich. I remember one day there was bad weather, so no flights. We were in our dugout, preparing for a dancing party. We were flying in padded pants and Canadian flight jackets. I couldn't go dancing like that, but where were my smart uniform trousers? I couldn't find them anywhere! And so I went to see Aksentievich, who issued pilots with replacement kit: 'Peter Aksentievich, have you seen my trousers?' – 'What did they look like?' – 'Dark-blue ones.' – 'Do you remember I bought half a litre of vodka two days ago? Those were your trousers.' There were few alcoholics like that.

I didn't drink or smoke during the war. Drinking alcohol makes me feel sick so I used to give my vodka ration to the other pilots: later I'd receive a chocolate bar instead of vodka. One of our technicians managed to get a barrel of pure alcohol when we were about to leave for the Winter War with Finland. The temperatures were so low that the vodka froze! It was sent in small bottles of 100 grams. If the temperature was minus 40 degrees there were crystals of ice in the bottle. In that case the bottle had to be warmed up in the hand and then consumed.

At that time we flew R-5s with open canopies. We had special face masks with holes for eyes and were supposed to wear flight goggles too, but they'd get covered in condensation so we flew without them, sheltering behind the cockpit's windscreen. My nose and my hands were frostbitten! Before flying north my technician told me: 'You have to take a shot, otherwise you'll die. You have to drink pure alcohol, not this nasty vodka. Pour a drop into your glass, drink, inhale and chase it with water. OK?' I agreed and he poured pure alcohol for me. I drank it but could neither inhale nor exhale! He told me: 'Here, take a glass of water.' But he made a mistake and poured vodka instead of water. What a nightmare – I almost died! At the same time I realized that drinking was not my thing.

I could relax without vodka, even after battles. We had good times with the guys, making jokes and organizing dance parties. We received a whole regiment of girls later in the war. All men were taken into the infantry, so we had girls in our ground support units. A dance troupe visited us once when we were in Afrikanda. They were bombed on the way: no one was killed but they arrived badly shaken. After recovering their composure they gave a concert. Afterwards a dinner with music was prepared. There was plenty of alcohol so our guys got drunk and started shooting. Panic broke out! I tried to calm the dancers' nerves: 'Relax, the Guards are just having fun!'

What else can I you tell about our life at the front? We didn't have any special superstitions. True, we didn't take pictures before take off, but then we didn't take a lot of pictures anyway. But we shaved as normal – no superstitions related to that – nor did we have any special talismans.

Our uniforms? We were very proud of our shoulder-boards. Our shoulder-boards were wide, while those of ground personnel were narrow. Once a girl was dancing with a doctor. She touched his shoulder-boards and said: 'Narrow shoulder-boards, no good for me!'

Did we have love affairs at the front? Of course we did! I had so many problems from them!

Did political work take up a lot of time? No. We had a case when a secretary from some Party committee was sent to us as a *politruk*. He wasn't a pilot – just a peasant guy. So, when the Western Allies opened the second front a meeting was arranged. They spoke a lot about how Eisenhower's forces had finally landed in France and so on. This committee secretary also spoke, saying: 'Comrades, at last the Western Allies are helping us by opening the second front under the leadership of General Ezenaher . . .' All the pilots fell on the floor with laughter and forever afterwards the *Politruk* was dubbed 'Ezenaher' [this word sounds similar to 'na her', the short form of 'poshel na her' or 'fuck off' – Ed.]. Such was the political work! No, it didn't create problems. It was quite OK.

* * *

Did we use gun cameras? Yes, we had them. The camera had a delay and if you let the trigger go, the machine guns wouldn't fire but a camera would work for several more seconds in order to catch the result. When a fast-paced battle took place you wouldn't see anything anyway: that's why 'kills' were mostly confirmed by ground troops and air observation posts (or if you flew in a group, by the other pilots). But HQ didn't always believe us and scouts would be sent to confirm our claims. If we scored a victory over the sea, there was no one to confirm it.

We had a unique rule in our regiment. If a group shot down a plane the victory was attributed to every pilot in the group. That's why I have 26 shared victories and only four individual victories. Do you see? We were not hunting individual victories: the main thing was to preserve the lives of one's comrades. Of course, counting shared victories made it look like all our pilots had high tallies, when in fact we didn't shoot down many planes. But attributing a victory to all pilots in the group preserved friendly relations and the spirit of collectivism, while discouraging any thoughts of becoming an individual hero. And yet, of course, there were ambitious pilots who wanted to score more. For example, Krivosheev always tried to score individual victories for himself. We tried our best to cover him but in vain – he was shot down and killed.

How did I score four individual victories? For example, we flew four in a group. We were still flying LaGGs then. I had an excellent plane, an early production model, well polished, almost black with camouflage paint. I called it a 'Cobra' although we didn't have Cobras at that time. I've already mentioned that I had very good eyesight: well, I spotted a German scout plane. Kutakhov told me: 'If you see him, go for him!' I climbed up to 6,000m without an oxygen mask! We'd normally fly low but in this case I had to climb to get that scout. I flew along the railway and finally caught up with this Dornier 215. At first he didn't see me, flying a straight course and taking pictures. Then a German rear gunner spotted me and opened fire. I manoeuvred, in order to get closer to the scout, and hit him with all my weapons. He smoked, started a dive, and I followed him all the way until he crashed.

Once I was sent alone to escort a Pe-2 on a reconnaissance mission. We were already on the way back, me flying behind and on the sunny side. Two Germans came out of nowhere. They chased the Pe-2 and didn't notice me. I dived from above and downed one of them before the very eyes of the Pe-2's crew. The second Fritz quit. This victory was counted but sometimes it was very hard to confirm a 'kill': you shoot down a plane and there are no troops on the ground, no one saw it fall.

Our 145th Fighter Regiment was better trained than the sister 147th (by now we'd been renamed the 19th and 20th Guards Fighter Regiments, respectively), which took much higher losses than we did: so in August 1942 I was transferred to strengthen the regiment. I didn't want to go, but Turkin, Commander of the Fourteenth Army, sent a U-2 plane with a direct order: 'Tie up Gaidaenko and take him to the 20th Guards Regiment.' What could I do? Well, there were no 'old hands' left in the 20th Guards when I arrived, only young boys straight from the academies. Now, there are a lot of lies about our losses: but the fact remains that the Germans beat us up real good! Why? Judge for yourself. The 20th Guards had just been transferred from Murmashi to Shongui for retraining. I took over a squadron. Do you know what sort of personnel it had? My deputy was a captain who'd received a ten-year jail sentence for cowardice! But they sent him to the front instead, implying that one more act of cowardice would result in transfer to a penal battalion. Meanwhile, the other pilots were NCOs straight from academies in ankle boots, leg wrappings and thin little overcoats. I interviewed them and asked: 'How many hours of flying do you have?' One of them explained: 'We flew I-16s, I'm the most experienced with ten solo flights. The rest made four or five solo flights.' How could one send pilots like that into battle?!

Do you know how they trained our pilots? In the early war they forbade aerobatics! When I was retraining for I-16s I asked Novozhilov: 'Show me how to fight; I don't know anything about aerobatics.' He replied: 'First, aerobatics are forbidden. Second, if you get in a dogfight you must learn how to manoeuvre as best you can: if you don't they'll shoot you down.' Quite a lesson! I had at least some experience – long hours spent flying night and day – but those guys from the academy, they needed at least one more year of training! Later in the war so-called 'reserve air regiments' were formed. Training in those regiments was also insufficient. They were supposed to teach dogfights and so on, but the personnel of the reserve regiments complained they had no fuel and no spare parts for planes, as everything was sent to the front.

The 20th Regiment was flying Kittyhawks. These sergeants had to be retrained for them. The Kittyhawk was a complicated plane. During take off, if you pulled the stick sharply, in order to lift the tail, it would turn to the side. The same thing happened during landing. As soon as it started turning, the Kittyhawk would roll and the console would break. Every flight these young pilots wrecked the planes! Later I managed to escape from this regiment. What could I do with those NCOs? I'd have been killed! I picked four better pilots and moved back to my old regiment, where I led the 3rd Squadron.

A bit later in the war we tried to train inexperienced pilots in the following way. We'd put one 'green' pilot in a group of six or eight planes. Even with this tactic we had an incident. We took one 'green' guy as wingman for Squadron Commander Mironenko. A dogfight started. The 'green' pilot completely lost his mind, got on Mironenko's tail, and opened fire on him! He could no longer tell a German plane from a Russian! We yelled at him over the radio, but in the middle of a battle there was no time to stop him, and this guy was gunning his own comrades! Finally a Fritz shot him down.

* * *

The most intense air battles in the north took place in 1941–42, when the Germans were going for Murmansk. After that it was just small skirmishes. But there were still losses, like Ivan Bochkov, who was a good guy. Ivan was in the 147th Regiment before the war and was considered a poor pilot, though he didn't cause trouble. They told me he'd been very downcast. He had a cute wife but – and I beg your pardon – also a whore. She slept with everyone. Well, when the war started all families were evacuated and with his wife out of the way Ivan began flying well. He was a handsome guy, a lot of girls were interested in him, but he was a modest person in this respect. He fought well, receiving the Gold Star of a 'Hero of the Soviet Union', but was killed. I don't know how it happened.

Besides that, I was shot down for the second time in 1942 and had to crash land in a forest, breaking my spine in the process. The good thing was that I crashed near our airfield and they started looking for me right away. If they hadn't found me I'd have probably frozen to death, as I was unable to move. Now they say the NKVD guys were bad, but our SMERSh officer – a former engineer from Leningrad – was a decent officer. I was friends with him till his very death. He led the search group that found and rescued me. While I was away, Regimental Commander Novozhilov almost got my entire squadron killed on 12 March 1943. I'll go back a bit in my story . . .

At the very beginning of the war our regimental commander was Nikolai I Shmelkov, but he didn't stay long and the next commander was Georgi I. Reifschneider. He didn't fly a lot but he was a great organizer of operations. He was the first to introduce debriefings and to develop tactics in consultation with pilots. He didn't give orders but allowed pilots the chance to make their own decisions. That's why, during his term, the regiment greatly improved. In mid-1942 Reifschneider changed his last name to Kalugin and was promoted to *Shturmovik* divisional commander. We had a joke then. One pilot says: 'Our Divisional Commander is Kalugin, a very smart guy.' The other one replies: 'Your Kalugin looks just like our Reifschneider!' We asked them to make Kutakhov our regimental commander but Novozhilov was appointed instead. He was a *kolkhoz* peasant, already an old person at that time. He was afraid of his superiors and blindly followed orders without even thinking. One day he was called at his CP and ordered to scramble a squadron. He fired a signal flare for take off, not caring that German fighters were all around. Four guys were shot down at take off. Now, some say German pilots were 'knights'. My wingman was Ivchenko, a tall and good-looking guy (I transferred him from the 20th Regiment), and once he crash landed on a frozen lake. When you make a crash landing you have to hide behind your plane, but Ivchenko ran away: the Nazis shot him on the ground – what a knightly act!

After I was shot down I was grounded for a long time, stuck in various hospitals. There were not so many medical inspections those days: if you didn't make it clear you couldn't fly, they'd just let you carry on. I recovered some, returned to the regiment, and started flying little by little. It was hard at the beginning. I didn't fly battle missions, but I went to Krasnoyarsk twice to ferry Cobras to the front. Later I went back to normal battle activities and everything was all right. After a while I was appointed a divisional aerobatics inspector and later a commander of the 152nd Regiment.

* * *

German pilots? They were very good and well trained. Their planes were also of high quality. But we managed to shoot them down, so they must have had their shortcomings. I'd like to note that the Germans did not fight like us. We'd engage the enemy outnumbered six-to-one if ordered to; but the Germans never fought in such situations: if they were outnumbered they simply quit. I don't know about other theatres of operations, but that's what it was like in mine. They would also dodge an engagement if we had altitude superiority. But they were good fighters. Unfortunately we had very little information about the German pilots opposing us and were never given a chance to talk to captured pilots.

Were there cases of cowardice in the squadron? Our pilot Peter Aksentievich was a bit of a coward. For example, when we were retraining for Cobras in Afrikanda, he flew to Alakurtti. Well, he was flying at high altitude, there was no one around, and the Cobra had a good radio. Back at HQ Aksentievich's voice came over the receiver: 'Messers, come out, Peter Aksentievich is above you!' Kutakhov was standing with the microphone in his hand and shouted: '109s behind you!' Peter Aksentievich shut up and his Cobra came flying in at low altitude twenty minutes later. It was decided that he should be removed from the regiment.

What can I say about Kutakhov?[3] He was an excellent pilot but with a bad temper. I remember the 837th Regiment arriving with Hurricanes (awful planes – very nasty). We called that regiment a 'zoo' because all their planes were painted with tigers, lions and bears. They landed in Murmashi and we were in Shongui. Kutakhov was considered an experienced pilot and our Commander ordered him to fly to Murmashi to brief the newly arrived flyers about the theatre of operations. When the pilots were assembled for briefing it was announced: 'Here is local Squadron Commander Kutakhov and he will tell you about the theatre of operations.' Some of the pilots whispered: 'Who's he? Don't we know already how to fight?' Kutakhov heard this and lost his temper: 'Is that right? Well, fuck you all!' He turned around, grabbed his flying helmet, and flew away. Two days later the 'zoo' regiment was destroyed, blown into pieces. The surviving pilots were sent to us without planes. One of them was in our squadron. He was a Muscovite from a genteel family. All our pilots were quite crude and regularly used all kinds of obscenities. That guy blushed even from our curses. But later he got used to it, flew well, and survived the war.

Well, Kutakhov was different: he could curse you and even hit you in the face if he thought it was necessary. But when it came to air battles, he was a real warrior and could lead his regiment. Few men could do that. I had good relations with him but can't say I received any privileges from him. After the war, when he became Deputy Commander-in-Chief and then Commander-in-Chief of the Air Force, his negative features came forward: his ambition and preference for bootlickers. He really loved all kinds of gifts and I always disliked this.

What did the war mean to me? It was a hard duty. Of course I was happy when it was over. I didn't enjoy fighting at all. When I scored a victory it felt nice, but I wouldn't say I wanted to repeat the experience over and over again. I just wanted to fly.

Notes

1. Paulina Denisovna Dudnik Ossipenko (1907–39) was one of several female pilots who broke world records for women's long-distance flight in the late 1930s.

2. The Bell Airacobra (known in Britain as the 'Aircobra') was a US single-seat fighter, which briefly entered service with the British RAF in October 1941. Several versions of the plane (designated P-39 by the USAAF) were manufactured between 1939–44 and some 5,000 were supplied to the USSR under Lend/Lease.
3. Pavel Stepanovich Kutakhov became Commander-in-Chief of Soviet Air Forces in March 1969. A 'Hero of the Soviet Union', Kutakhov scored some 13 individual victories and 28 shared victories on the Karelian Front during the Great Patriotic War.

Fighter Aircraft on the Eastern Front

Nikolai G. Golodnikov Interviewed by Andrei Sukhrukov

I met first Nikolai G. Golodnikov in the autumn of 2000. I was surprised by his appearance, for he looked much younger than his 80 years. At first he was suspicious – because I am not an academic or a trained journalist – but in the event granted me several lengthy interviews, the results of which are given below.

Golodnikov graduated from the Eisk Military Naval Pilot Academy three days before *Barbarossa* plunged the Soviet Union into the Second World War. A first-rate student, he initially remained in the academy as a flight instructor, before transferring to the front in March 1942. Appointed a pilot in the 72nd Mixed Air Regiment of the Northern Red Banner Fleet's Air Arm (later becoming the 2nd Guards Fighter Regiment under B.F. Safonov), Golodnikov fought the whole war with this unit, rising to senior pilot, wing commander and deputy squadron commander. After the war he became a squadron commander.

The Hawker Hurricane

British pilots flew alongside N.G. Golodnikov's 2nd Guards Fighter Regiment on the Eastern Front for a time, and British Hawker Hurricanes were later supplied to the Soviets. I asked N.G. Golodnikov his views on the British pilots and the Hurricanes they bequeathed . . .

The 151st RAF Wing flew in from an aircraft carrier. The pilots were of varying level. The strongest squadron under a man named Miller, having good flying skills and teamwork. But a Hurricane is still a Hurricane, and from September 1941 to May 1942, if I remember correctly, they lost five pilots and downed 12 Germans. The two other squadrons were weaker. But the British were brave pilots. They never tried to evade a battle. They attacked well. Any Russian fighter regiment would take Miller's squadron altogether and would not be disappointed. They were strong guys.

Miller's squadron flew all important missions with us. How did we communicate in the air? Was there something to communicate about?! The flight plan was worked out on the ground, zones of responsibility were assigned, basic variants in case of repelling attacks were also worked out ('you go here, we go there'), so what could we discuss in the air? Everyone knew what to do without words.

Eventually the 151st RAF Wing passed on their own Hurricanes to us and we studied them. Although there were British instructors, there were no two-seater trainers, and all the manuals were in English, so they sent us female translators. But even then the instructor would simply show the cockpit to a small group, which was then supposed to pass the information on to all the others. Actually, it turned out the British had a certain Major Rook who, having graduated from our Kachinsk Air School, could speak Russian quite well. But he only began speaking Russian at a farewell party – during training he had spoken English only! He said at the party: 'I could not speak Russian as I was an official and I had my orders.' Our Squadron Commander Kovalenko had studied with Major Rook and tried to persuade him into speaking Russian: 'Why are you cheating? You understand all we say!' But the Brit would only speak English. This Rook flew an I-16 once. Upon landing he climbed out drenched with sweat: 'Let the Russians fly it!' was his only comment.

We retrained on Hurricanes squadron by squadron. It took us about five days to do it. We studied general design: 'The engine is here, you refuel through this one, oil system is here,' and so on. We didn't go into all the details. We'd talk, sit in a cockpit for a while, taxi a couple of times, and then take off. After three flights we were officially retrained. As our saying goes: 'If you want to live, you will land.' Safonov was the first one to take off. First he sat in the cockpit for some four hours, so his hands 'could get used to the plane', then he took off and the others followed.

We had two types of Hurricane: one with eight machine guns and one with 12. There were no other differences between them. Then we started to receive the planes in boxes straight from England. They must have been bound for the Sahara, as they were painted in desert yellow camouflage!

My first impression of a Hurricane was that it had a 'hump'! Such a humpback could not be a good fighter! This impression didn't change later on. I was especially amazed at the thick wings, which were thicker than those of a Pe-2 bomber. The Hurricane was easier to fly than the I-16 and we didn't have any trouble learning how to control it.

The Hurricane's cockpit, of course, was larger than the I-16 and forward visibility was very good. But to the side, and especially to the rear, it was poor. The canopy reminded me of an I-16: it had many sections and slid backwards. The many sections greatly hindered lateral visibility: anywhere you tried to stick your nose the view was blocked by a glazing-bar. At first we slid the canopy open before combat, in order to improve visibility. Later, when we were more familiar with the canopy, we left it closed so as not to lose speed.

The Hurricane's control stick was a surprise. It was like a bomber stick. The upper portion was thick and had a ring, inside of which were two triggers, which looked like switches. In order to fire all the weapons, one had to use both hands. At its base the stick moved only forward and backward; right or left movement was accomplished at the mid-stick level, from which cables controlled the ailerons.

The Hurricane had reliable armoured glass, and the back of the seat was also armoured. The control panel did not cause any problems. Of course, all measurements were in pounds and feet, but we quickly got used to it. We had exactly the same location of indicators on a UT-2 plane, in metric system, of course, so those who'd flown a UT-2 had an easy time adapting.

We had experienced pilots and you would sometimes ask them: 'What's this indicator?' They'd reply: 'Don't pay attention to it. You will not need it in real life. Here is altitude, RPM, oil pressure, temperature – that's enough.'

The Hurricane had ultra-high frequency radios with six channels. They were reliable and good sets with both receiver and transmitter. The only negative aspect of this was that the microphone was inside the oxygen mask, making it heavy and cumbersome in combat. If you wore the mask too tight it pinched, and if you loosened it, G-forces pulled it off! The transmitter was simplex-duplex, which means that it could be activated to send or receive with a push-to-talk switch and also with voice. When we spoke the transmitter turned on automatically, and when we were silent we could listen. We could select the mode ourselves. We had a special knob in the cockpit that we could place on voice-activate or push-to-talk. In the beginning we all used the voice-activation capability. Sometimes, in combat someone would start cursing: 'Damn you, Fritz . . .' and the transmitter would switch on, stopping the pilot from receiving, while the other pilots were unable to transmit commands. Later we were ordered to switch to push-to-talk control on all aircraft. It was placed on the throttle control, and we wired down the knob for voice-activation. Because of the microphone the oxygen mask was always on our faces. The oxygen supply system was reliable.

The Hurricane's landing gear worked well: it was retracted automatically with hydraulics by a special lever. This same lever was used to control the flaps. And the plane had 8 and 12 machine guns, four or six in each wing. Those were 7.7mm Browning machine guns. They were comparable with ShKAS in terms of reliability, but they often failed due to dust. We tackled the problem like this: we glued percale on all the machine-gun holes, and when you opened fire bullets went right through. The machine guns became reliable then. They were of low efficiency when fired from distances of 150–300m.

On the initiative of B.F. Safonov, our Regimental Commander, the regiment's mobile aircraft repair workshop started mounting Soviet-made weapons in our Hurricanes. We had an armaments engineer, Boris Sobolevsky, who supervised this effort. We had many other skilful craftsmen as well. They mounted either two ShVAKs in each wing or one ShVAK and one Berezin. Later, the British filed a complaint against us – how could we do such a thing without their permission – and so on. Bullshit. Everyone knew they did this to cover their backs in case of trouble. As for the Lewis machine guns, I'd say that if you got close enough, they could do a lot of damage as well.

My Squadron Commander was Alexander A. Kovalenko (he passed away recently, may he rest in peace), one of our first pilots to become a 'Hero of the Soviet Union'. He was a typical Ukrainian, thoughtful and quiet. I was his wingman. I think this happened in 1942. There was a large-scale German air raid on Murmansk and six of us were scrambled. They told us on the radio from the ground: 'Zero One! Group of 109s!' I had a good sight of the air space and reported to Kovalenko: 'I see the 109s!' He quietly replied, 'Fine. Let's go beat the 109s.' The next message from the ground station: 'Zero One! Group of 87s! Switch over to the 87s!' Again he quietly said, 'Let's go beat the 87s.' We spotted them on the approaches to Murmansk. There were about 20 of them, perhaps more. We attacked them from below at high speed. I watched as Kovalenko placed his Hurricane almost vertical and with a skid, opened up on a *Stuka* from about 50m with 12 machine guns. Then as Kovalenko fell away, I followed him and saw the tail of the Junkers flying in one direction and the rest of the plane in another. Kovalenko had sliced the *Stuka* in half before my eyes. Kovalenko's only comment was: 'I spent almost all my ammo!' The ground station later informed us that the Germans were screaming: 'We're surrounded by Soviet fighters! They are killing us!' Along with the other six fighters who engaged the Messers, we shot down eight aircraft on that day.

By the way, I scored my first victory in a Hurricane, against a Bf 109. My aircraft still had English weapons. I was a wing-man then, and the Fritz was attacking my leader but didn't make it. He got between me and my leader, and I cut him down from 15–20m.

As for the Hurricane's engine, it was powerful as such, but it couldn't stand long periods of work at maximum regimes and would quickly break down. The engine worked very clean, it had exhaust stacks and flame suppressors, mounted like mufflers. This was very comfortable as the flames did not blind the pilot. Our planes were much worse in this respect. But at negative G-forces the engine choked. There was no compensating tank. This was very bad because we had to execute any manoeuvre with positive G-forces. We learnt this peculiarity quickly, but initially, in the heat of battle, we would forget about it. Later, with experience, we never permitted such a situation to happen, as an abrupt fall in the engine's output would unexpectedly alter the manoeuvre, which was dangerous in combat.

The Hurricane had the same maximum altitude as the I-16. It had a propeller with controllable pitch, but with wooden blades. Pitch was changed manually, with levers, which was not hard. Each flight had one technician to maintain the propellers, one person for four planes. The airframe was unimpressive, too heavy. Of course, the engine was too weak for such an airframe. There was enough fuel for 1 hour 20 minutes or 1 hour 30 minutes.

I should mention one more thing about the airframe. The Hurricane had a very light tail. We were flying from sandy, insufficiently solid airfields. A technician or mechanic had to sit on the tail; we had to taxi with a passenger on the tail. We even took off with a technician sitting on the tail! We had a technician called Rudenko who flew a circle around the airfield sitting on the tail. He didn't jump off in time so he made holes in the skin of the stabilizer and sat there. Happily the pilot landed with him, but there were cases when men fell off and got killed.

Although the Hurricane was on a par with the I-16 (Types 10, 17 and 21) I just didn't like it. It didn't touch my heart. Marshal G.V. Zimin wrote in his memoirs that: 'fighting in a Hurricane was the same as fighting flying a pterodactyl.' It was unique, he said, from an aerodynamic point of view: it didn't gain speed in a dive and immediately lost speed in a climb. I agree with him. The Hurricane was just like a pterodactyl. It had a very thick profile and poor acceleration characteristics. At maximum speed it was probably somewhat faster than an I-16, but many things could happen before it reached that speed. It was not slow in responding to the control stick, but everything happened smoothly, slowly. In the I-16, if you moved the stick, the plane flipped over right away, while this humpback was very slow. But it had good lifting strength and was therefore comparable to the I-16 in rate of climb. It was very good in horizontal manoeuvrability. If four Hurricanes established a circle, it was impossible to break up this formation. No Germans could break into the circle either.

But the Hurricane was very poor in vertical manoeuvre, due to thick wing profile. We mostly tried to impose a battle in the horizontal plane and would not go into a vertical one. The Hurricane had a short take-off run, also because of its thick wings. In its characteristics the Hurricane was somewhat inferior to the Messerschmitt Bf 109E, mostly in vertical manoeuvre, but was not inferior in the horizontal. When the Bf 109F arrived the Hurricane was outclassed, but we continued to fight the war on them. The Hurricane burned rapidly – and to cinders like a match – as it had durale covering only on the tail and wings, the rest was percale. The I-16 did not burn so ferociously. I flew about 20 sorties on Hurricanes and fought three or four dogfights. Then I switched to the P-40.

The Curtiss P-40 (Tomahawk and Kittyhawk)

In production between 1939–44 the American Curtiss P-40 was known as the 'Warhawk' to the USAAF and the 'Tomahawk' and 'Kittyhawk' to the RAF. Supplied to the Soviets under the terms of Lend/Lease, I asked G.N. Golodnikov how the fighter compared to the Russian I-16 and the British Hawker Hurricane, and to give an example of the plane's capabilities in action …

Of course the P-40s were better than the I-16 and the Hurricane. After the first flight I said to myself: 'Well, Kolya, finally you too have a modern fighter!'

The cockpit was vast and high. At first it felt unpleasant to sit waist-high in glass, as the edge of the fuselage was almost at waist level. But the bullet-proof glass and armoured seat were strong and visibility was good.

The control stick was almost like that of our fighters, with machine-gun triggers, and close by was a trigger that was used to lower and raise the main gear and flaps. The radio set was also good. It was powerful, reliable, but only on HF (high frequency). When Safonov began flying in a Tomahawk he had a Hurricane radio installed because half of the regiment was still flying Hurricanes, which had UHF radios. So he flew with two radios. The American radios did not have hand microphones but throat microphones. These were good throat mikes: small, light and comfortable.

Our Tomahawks and Kittyhawks had different armaments. Tomahawks were armed with four machine guns – two synchronized and two in the wings. I don't remember which machine guns we had in the wings, as they were soon removed to lighten the plane, while the synchronized machine guns were Browning 12.7mm – powerful and reliable. Kittyhawks had six wing machine guns, also Brownings 12.7mm. After some time, rather soon, we dismounted a couple of machine guns on the Kittyhawks as well, fighting with four machine guns. The absence of cannon was not a tragedy for us. When we had Tomahawks with just two machine guns, of course, we longed for more firepower. Kittyhawks had four, which was enough for me. Of course, it demanded fire from short distance, from point-blank range.

Later they began to employ many P-40s as mast-top and light bombers. Our regiment had an air cover mission and our sister 78th Fighter Regiment was given mast-top bombing and ground support missions. When we began to receive P-39 Cobras we gave them our P-40s. The maintenance personnel installed Soviet-made bomb consoles on their P-40s to fit our bombs. To be more precise, the technicians replaced the American bomb consoles because Soviet bombs could not be hung on them. I recall that the fuselage bomb console was dual-purpose: you could hang a bomb or an auxiliary fuel tank.

The P-40 carried a good bomb load – 450kg. This meant a FAB-100 under each wing and an FAB-250 under the fuselage. When our comrades from the 78th Regiment flew with a bomb load we had to provide air cover till the moment they dropped their bombs, after which they could kill anyone themselves.

The gunsight was an American-made collimator sight. It was OK. We didn't mount any Soviet equipment on P-40s except the bomb consoles.

Tomahawks had the Allison engine – not very good but powerful as such. As one pushed it to full RPMs, toward maximum output, it would begin to 'make metal dust'. Apparently this was our fault because, as we were told, we lacked 'oil culture'. Later the Americans modified the powerplant and the Kittyhawks received more powerful and reliable engines. In terms of horsepower it would have been nice to have a stronger engine in the P-40 airframe, but we only started noticing lack of thrust-to-weight ratio in late 1943.

I say again that the P-40 significantly outclassed the Hurricane and completely outclassed the I-16. Actually, the P-40 could engage all Messerschmitts on equal terms, almost to the end of 1943. If you take into consideration all the characteristics of the P-40, then the Tomahawk was equal to the Bf 109F and the Kittyhawk was slightly above it. Its speed and vertical and horizontal manoeuvre were good and fully competitive with enemy aircraft. Acceleration rate was a bit low, but when you got used to the engine, it was OK. We considered the P-40 a decent fighter plane.

An example of the P-40 in action? One time we were flying Tomahawks. Four of us engaged six Bf 109Fs and shot down three without losing one of our own. We did this employing correct tactics and the aircraft did not fail us. Here's how it went. We were flying at an altitude of 3,000–4,000m. The Germans in the Bf 109Fs were 500m lower. We attacked them with surprise, out of the sun, at a good speed. They never saw us. We shot down two in the first pass, leaving four. They reacted appropriately, dispersing in pairs and attempting to engage us in battle in the vertical plane, counting on the superiority of the Messer in this manoeuvre. We also split up and entered the battle 'pair versus pair'. This was our kind of fight! We shot down the third right away, since the P-40 did not lag behind in the vertical (we had a good reserve of speed) and was superior to the Messer in horizontal combat. Their will to fight quickly left them. They split up, went to full power, and broke away in a steep dive.

If we'd been flying Hurricanes, we wouldn't have been able to impose such an active and aggressive combat. The main strength of the P-40 was its speed.

I shot down a Bf 109F. I was a wingman and the German pilot attacked my leader. He failed to see me or just didn't take me into account (I think that he just didn't see me). I noticed him from far away. I saw him attacking my leader. I had quite good experience and knew the habits of German pilots well. If I'd been less experienced, I'd have opened covering fire, just repelled the German, but I decided to shoot him down. I calculated when he would open fire and planned my manoeuvre so that I'd catch him. Of course it was a serious risk. If I made a mistake, I would have lost my leader – an infamy that would always live with you! So I had to manoeuvre in a way that I'd not lose my leader and open covering fire at any moment. In general, when the German was in the position to open fire 100m behind my leader, I was 25m behind the German. I opened fire: two large-calibre machine guns at point-blank range. It sounds like a long story to tell, but in battle this all lasted just a few seconds.

I was also seriously shot up in a P-40, but I made it back to my airfield. I was leader of a pair of Tomahawks escorting *Shturmoviks* and we flew into Messers. I saw a pair of Messers starting an attack and charged them head on. I fired from a very unfavourable angle, but I fired a short burst, not to hit, but to give a clear signal: 'I see you, get lost!'

Normally the Germans would get lost, but in this case I saw that the leading German fighter was covered by a small cloud of smoke, which meant he'd opened fire. Next thing I saw was a flash, explosion and smoke! I was dumbfounded for several seconds and then regained my senses. I flew on, my plane shivered, the whole control panel was blown to pieces with shrapnel. I pulled the stick and tried the pedals – the plane was still under control, but the trimmer didn't work.

But why was the plane shaking? It turned out that the propeller pitch switched and I couldn't decrease it. I decreased RPMs, turned around, and flew back to my airfield at treetop level. It turned out the Messer hit me with two rounds. The first hit the propeller and knocked out the pitch control mechanism, while the second hit the left side of the cockpit. It was only on the ground that I realized that the left side of my body (mostly my arm and leg) were peppered with small splinters. I had about 100 of them in me. When I was flying, I didn't even feel any pain. I knew I was wounded but I thought it only slight. I was rescued by an interesting design feature of P-40. Its trimmer was guided by a large (8–10 cm) and thick (1.5–2 cm) steel gear, and controlling cable would go to the trimmers from that gear. This gear was just at my left arm. That very gear was hit. The round didn't penetrate the gear, and this is why all splinters flew along the cockpit, not into it. I was only hit by a small portion of splinters.

They took me to Severomorsk, to an Air Force hospital. They removed the larger splinters but the small ones are still inside me. Thank God there were almost no deep wounds. I spent several days in the hospital and then they brought the survivors from the PQ-17 convoy, most of them were frostbitten. All hospitals were full of them those days. They asked me if I'd like to go to the medical unit of my regiment as every bed was precious. Of course, I was all for it! As soon as I returned, I continued flying right away, without any further treatment. I was an experienced pilot, not a 'green', so who would fight the war for me?

The Bell P-39 (Airacobra)

The Airacobra (dubbed 'Aircobra' by the British) was designed by the American Bell company, some 5,000 being supplied to the USSR under the terms of Lend/Lease. I asked N.G. Golodnikov when he began flying P-39s and how he liked this aircraft ...

I started flying Cobras in November 1942. We received the first batch from Moscow, in containers. We assembled them and then learnt to fly them. Those were P-39Qs, perhaps Types 1 and 2, from the British order. They had yellow camouflage.

Training was thorough. We had instructors and all sorts of manuals and textbooks. Retraining was done quickly, in five or six days. Later they flew Cobras to us or we picked them up in Krasnoyarsk. These were Types Q-5, -10, -25, -30, and Q-35. These aircraft were made especially for the USSR. We fought the remaining period of the war only in Q models.

I liked the Cobra, especially the Q-5 version. It was the lightest version of all Cobras and was the best fighter I ever flew.

The cockpit seemed a bit small after the P-40, but it was very comfortable, and visibility was outstanding. The instrument panel was very ergonomic, with the entire complement of instruments right up to an artificial horizon and radio compass. It even had a relief tube, in the shape of a funnel. If you wanted to piss, pull the tube out from under the seat and go for it! It even had holders for pens and pencils. The armoured glass was very strong, extremely thick. The armour on the back of the seat was also thick. The first models had armoured glass in front and rear, but the armoured seat lacked a head protector (the rear armoured glass compensated for it). In the later models, starting with Q-25, there was no armoured rear glass but the armoured seat was equipped with a head protector. The oxygen equipment was reliable, although the mask was quite small, only covering the nose and mouth. We wore this mask only at high altitude. The HF radio set was powerful, reliable and clear.

The first Cobras we received from Moscow had a 20mm Hispano-Suiza cannon and two heavy Browning machine guns, synchronized and mounted in the nose. Later, Cobras arrived with the M-4 37mm cannon and four machine guns, two synchronized and two wing-mounted. We immediately removed the wing machine guns, leaving one cannon and two machine guns. I can't say that a 37mm gun was a clear advantage or disadvantage. The M-4 had its strengths and weaknesses. You had to take advantage of the strengths and play down the weaknesses. The former included powerful rounds and a reliable action; the latter included a low rate of fire (just three rounds a second) and low ammo storage (30 rounds only).

The Cobras had interesting reloading and trigger mechanisms for the cannon – they were hydraulic. At first, in the English variant of the Cobra, we had a lot of trouble with them, as hydraulics froze up. It seems that the Cobras had been intended for Africa, because the hydraulic fluid grew thick in the sub-zero temperatures and clogged up holes in hydraulic cylinders. Our technicians replaced the hydraulic fluid and enlarged the diameter of the holes. Then the reloading began to work normally. By the way, all these Cobras had problems related to freezing hydraulics, not just the reloading mechanism.

Our Cobras had Allison engines. They were powerful but unreliable, especially in the early Q-1 and Q-2 types. Nevertheless, Cobras – especially the Q-5 – were on a par with all German fighters, and perhaps superior. I flew more than 100 combat sorties in the Cobra, including 17 air combats. The Cobra was not inferior to German fighters in speed, acceleration or manoeuvrability. It was a very balanced aircraft and proved to be a very good fighter in our Air Force.

The Messerschmitt Bf 109 and the Focke-Wulf FW 190

Designed in the 1930s the Bf 109 was the mainstay of the Luftwaffe's fighter force. Produced in greater quantities than any other fighter in history, the 109 went through several models, including the 109D ('Dora'), 109E ('Emil'), 109F ('Friedrich') and 109G ('Gustav'). Known colloquially as the 'Me 109' (after its inventor, Willy Messerschmitt) and officially as the 'Bf 109' (after Bayerische Flugzeugwerke, the company that filed the design), many Soviet pilots referred to the plane as the 'Messer'.

The Focke-Wulf FW 190 was introduced in 1941 by a German Air Force eager to stay ahead of Allied fighter design. Designed by Kurt Tank, the FW 190 (erroneously dubbed a 'Fokker' by Soviet pilots) is believed by many to have been the best fighter of the Second World War. I asked N.G. Golodnikov his opinion of both the Bf 109 and the FW 190; whether or not they really did outclass Allied aircraft; and ultimately, how Soviet victory was achieved in the skies of the Eastern Front ...

The Germans had good fighters. They were powerful, fast, durable and manoeuvrable.

Regarding the Bf 109E I can say that in its tactical and technical characteristics it corresponded to the I-16 Type 28 and Type 29, while surpassing all earlier types of the I-16 and Hurricane. But it was inferior to the Yak-1, P-40, and P-39. According to the pilots of the 20th IAP, the Yak-1 was superior to the 'Emil' in all parameters. This fighter was beginning to show its age by 1942, although in the North they employed it almost to the beginning of 1943. Later they withdrew all of them in a matter of a week or two. Apparently they had begun to suffer very serious losses. Later we encountered only the Bf 109F, Bf 109G, and FW 190.

The Bf 109F was superior to the E across the board, being more modern. It was an unbelievably dynamic aircraft with good speed and vertical manoeuvrability. In the horizontal plane it was not as good. Its armaments were normal: a 20mm cannon and two machine guns. Overall, of course, it was superior to all types of the I-16 and the Hurricane. It was equal to the Yak-1 and P-40, and slightly inferior to the P-39.

The Bf 109G was a powerful aircraft, fast and very good in vertical manoeuvre. It was not bad in horizontal manoeuvre but it appeared late, only in 1943, when all our regiments had already been equipped with modern aircraft. Overall, in its tactical and technical characteristics, it was on a par with the Yak-1B (7B, 9), La-5, and P-39 Airacobra, and a bit better than the P-40.

The Fokker [FW 190 – Ed.] also was a powerful and fast aircraft, but as a fighter it was inferior to the Bf 109G. It did not accelerate as quickly and was not as capable in the vertical plane. In terms of acceleration speed the Fokker was indeed weak and in this aspect was inferior to most of our aircraft, except for the P-40 perhaps. The Fokker was extremely powerful and therefore was often employed as an attack aircraft armed with bombs.

I can say that the Fokker engine was significantly more durable and could take more damage than that of the Messer. If the Fokker lost two cylinders it could still fly. Though increased reliability and resistance to damage are characteristic for all radial engines in comparison to in-line engines, German engines were not quite at the level of our own in this regard. Our I-16 and La-5 could lose four cylinders and still make it home. The Fokker could not lose more than two and still fly.

German pilots liked frontal assaults on FW 190s due to the radial engine, using it as a shield. The plane had extremely powerful weapons: four 20mm guns and two machine guns. Knowing that your aircraft could withstand a couple of hits while your burst would blow your opponent to pieces gave a lot of assurance in a frontal assault! Soon, however, the Germans started evading frontal attacks on Cobras, this was obvious. We had a 37mm gun, so no engine would save you, and one hit was enough to kill you. In such a situation you had to have guts for a frontal assault – the engine was of little help. We had stronger guts than the Germans.

I had a case. We engaged four Fokkers head on. We were four against four. During a turn my wingman happened to be in front of me. I ordered him: 'You go first, I'll cover you!' He hit the leading Fokker up front with a cannon round. He hit him with one or maybe two rounds. The Fokker was blown to pieces. The remaining three dispersed and escaped. It all took several seconds.

The Fokker was very good in a dive – this is true of all German fighters. It must be said that the Bf 109G and FW 190 carried very powerful weapons, with five and six firing points respectively, for the most part cannon. This was a very strong aspect of German aircraft. Nevertheless, with regard to the FW 190, although it was a powerful fighter its combat qualities were not unique in any way. Overall, I got the impression the Germans had high expectations for this aircraft but definitely overestimated it.

For example, who ever gave them the idea that the Cobra was inferior to the Fokker in speed? But they believed it! At first the Germans were so confident in their speed superiority that after an attack, a Fokker would attempt to break away from us at full throttle at engine boost. You would catch up with him and pour it on him from above. He would huff and puff but couldn't break away. We quickly taught the Germans not to rely on their engine power boost. Later it became a rule with Fokkers to break off an attack or evade fire only by means of a steep dive, no other method.

The Fokker was also inferior to the Cobra in the vertical plane, although they initially attempted to contest it with us. But they had to quickly abandon that habit. I don't understand why they decided the Fokker could outperform the Cobra in the vertical plane.

The acceleration rate of the Fokker was another weakness. Later they attempted to plan their manoeuvres so they would not lose speed. But in a prolonged battle of manoeuvre a Fokker would lose against a Yak, Lavochkin or Cobra. He lost his speed and then it was over, as he could be shot down more than once while regaining speed.

Although the Fokker made a big impact on the Western Front it was employed as an interceptor, while in the East it was used as a front-line fighter. In the West, Fokkers were guided to their targets by radar: so by the time contact was made with the enemy, the Fokkers had managed to accelerate and gain altitude superiority. In this scenario the low acceleration rate of the Fokker didn't play a major role because it had already acquired speed and altitude. But on our front the Germans didn't have that level of radar support, as radar stations were not nearly as numerous. In fact both we and the Germans largely used visual means to detect the enemy. When there was no radar support, rate of acceleration played a crucial role, and the Fokker was quite average in this respect.

You know, reference books always state that the Germans had speed advantage and people judge accordingly. But it's a common mistake for those who have not been in the Air Force to confuse two quite distinct concepts: top speed and combat speed. Top speed, or maximum speed, is measured in ideal conditions – horizontal flight, fixed altitude, and so on. But combat speed involves all the variables inherent in a manoeuvrable aerial battle. And so when I mention speed, I mean combat speed, not maximum speed, which wasn't important. If I had to catch up with him? OK, I caught up with him, then what? If you'd accelerated a lot you had to slow down, otherwise you'd overfly your target. Also, it's very hard to hit anything at high speed: or to be more precise, it's difficult to score enough hits to down an opponent. It had to work like this: catch up – slow down – shoot – and full throttle again. The ability of an engine to accelerate a plane and slow it down in the shortest possible time is just a dynamic characteristic.

Many consider that if an aircraft has a high maximum speed, then its combat speed will also be high, but that's not always so. It happens that during the comparison of two types of fighters, one of them may have a higher maximum speed and the other a higher combat speed. Such factors as responsiveness of the engine and thrust-to-weight ratio have substantial influence on the combat speed. These are the same factors that provide for maximum acceleration.

You don't need to go far to find an example of this. We had the LaGG-3 fighter. I flew it myself. Well, in 1941 this aircraft had a greater top speed than the Yak-1. It had several indisputable advantages over the Yak in addition to its higher speed. The LaGG was more durable and harder to set on fire. In addition, the LaGG had stronger weapons. But you know what? Ask any pilot who fought in the war: 'Of the two fighters, the Yak and the LaGG, which would you prefer?' He will most certainly choose the Yak. Why? Because the Yak was a very dynamic aircraft with high responsiveness, while the LaGG was an 'iron'.

Here is another example. Between the I-16 Type 28 and the Bf 109E, the Messer had a higher top speed and the combat speeds of these two aircraft were practically equal. If one compares the Type 28 with the Hurricane, the Hurricane had higher maximum speed but the I-16 higher combat speed. The Hurricane was a very slow fighter.

So you have to see that it is wrong to compare fighters by reference characteristics quoted in books, there are too many nuances that cannot be accounted for.

You ask: 'Did we beat the Germans with sheer numbers or with skill?' Both! There is a school of thought now that maintains we did not need an Air Force of high numbers, only high quality. Those who argue this case don't know what they are speaking about! Numerical superiority with all other factors even – I mean quality of planes and training of pilots – is a great thing. It decides the victory. The Germans were winning the air war at first. Why? Tactics and radio – yes, of course. But what was the crucial thing? The Germans wielded numerical tactical and strategic superiority. Their very first strikes destroyed a huge number of our aircraft. In one place the Germans destroyed aircraft right on the airfields; in another they shot them down in dogfights; and finally we destroyed others that we could not evacuate. But there was another aspect, forgotten almost by everyone. The Germans captured huge supply depots, as well as production and maintenance facilities. This is why we felt such a lack of aircraft in the first part of the war. Production of the new aircraft types dropped sharply, while it was impossible to repair old ones in the quantities required by the front. That's it, there were no planes!

Thus the Germans gained numerical superiority and didn't give us a chance to get even. Battles were raging on – no breaks at all! Of course, there were losses on both sides, but the Germans replaced their losses much faster than us. They put us under such pressure, there was no time to catch our breath! There is no doubt that this was the highest level of military art demonstrated by the Germans.

And we rank and file pilots saw the outcome ourselves. For a regular pilot, strategic numerical superiority of the enemy means you are outnumbered in *every* dogfight. Even if you're a good pilot, try surviving a battle of six against twelve! OK, you escape from one and the next one kills you. And those twelve opponents are not worse pilots than you. On the contrary, they are aces, the best of the best. And yet, no matter how good the Germans were, we made it! We gained battle experience and achieved parity in numbers with them. As soon as we were numerically superior to them, the situation changed radically in our favour.

For example, if you send 1,000 planes against your enemy's 100, even if both sides are matched in quality, you must win. That's exactly what happened in the second half of the war. Our planes became as good as the Germans' and the experience and training of our pilots as high: so as soon as we gained numerical superiority our victory became imminent. In the end, the Germans failed to produce enough aircraft or train enough pilots to ensure victory – but we did. That's the deal.

Observations and Notes on Soviet Fighter Production on the Eve of *Barbarossa*

The Soviet Union entered the war with a large but technically inferior fighter force. This inferiority was unavoidable in a country that had only just embarked on a programme of industrialisation already completed by the USA and the countries of Western Europe.

By the mid-1920s the USSR was still an agrarian country with a large rural population. Scientists, technicians and engineers were scarce in a country largely made up of semi-literate farm workers. Consequently the aircraft industry (including vital non-ferrous metallurgy) was almost non-existent. Suffice to say that pre-Revolutionary Russia could not produce roll bearings, carburettors or electrical equipment for aircraft; while aluminium, rubber, and even copper wire had to be purchased abroad. Thus the Soviet aircraft industry and ancillary raw material industries were built literally from scratch. Nevertheless, the pace of development was breathtaking, and by the outbreak of the Second World War the Soviet Union had created the largest Air Force in the world.

Of course, given such a fast rate of development, compromises were unavoidable, as best use had to be made of cheap and accessible raw materials, equipment and technology. This meant that the most research-intensive branches of the industry – engine design, instrument technology, radio and electronics – were undernourished. Thus the Soviet Union failed to catch up with the West in these areas during the 1930s: the difference in starting conditions was too great and the time allotted by history too short.

The necessity of relying on timber, plywood and steel instead of aluminium and magnesium was a serious limitation. The weight of wooden airframes led to compromises in armament, armour, fuel and ammo storage. And yet no viable alternatives existed for Soviet engineers if their targets were to be met: for war clouds were gathering and time was pressing.

And yet the inferior quality of Soviet aircraft was compensated by superior production numbers. As early as 1942, despite the evacuation of three-quarters of its aircraft industry, the USSR produced 40 per cent more aircraft than Germany. And in the following year, after Germany had undertaken significant measures to increase production, Soviet production was still 29 per cent higher. Only in 1944 did the Third Reich manage to equal Soviet aircraft production, thanks to the total mobilization of resources across Occupied Europe: but by that time two-thirds of Germany's air strength was committed against the Anglo-American Allies.

It is also worth mentioning that the USSR was obliged to commit significantly fewer resources (workers, plant, electricity) than Germany for the production of each plane. To make the comparison even more impressive, one must consider that in 1944 over 40 per cent of Soviet aircraft workers were women, and over 10 per cent were teenagers under the age of 18.

These indicators demonstrate that Soviet aircraft were simpler, cheaper and easier to manufacture than those produced by Germany. Nevertheless, by mid-1944 the best Soviet aircraft – fighters such as the Yak-3, Yak-9U and La-7 – were superior to a whole range of German planes of the same class. This was achieved – despite cheap materials, archaic machinery and a poorly trained workforce – by a combination of powerful engines and advanced aerodynamic design.

The great achievements of the Soviet aircraft industry in difficult wartime conditions are indisputable. But the decisive factor was that red-starred fighters managed to triumph at low and medium altitudes, where ground assault aircraft (the *Shturmoviks* and *Peshkas*) – the main striking power at the front line – operated. This provided for successful sorties against German defensive positions, troop concentrations and communications, which in turn, facilitated the victorious advance of Soviet troops during the final stage of the war.

'Donkeys' and 'Seagulls'

On the eve of Operation *Barbarossa* the Western Border Military Districts of Leningrad, Baltic, Western Special, Kiev Special and Odessa fielded a fighter force of some 4,226 aircraft. The bulk of these (some 42 per cent) were I-16s – dubbed 'Ishak' ('Donkey') – developed in 1933 by N.N. Polikarpov's design bureau. On the basis of available information, one can conclude that about 40 per cent of these I-16s were up-to-date Type 24s and 29s, fitted with 900hp M-63 engines. About 20 per cent were old, worn out Type 5 and 10 'Donkeys' with weaker 730hp M-25B engines. A similar number of cannon-armed Type 17s, 27s and 28s were also on strength. The remaining 20 per cent were two-seater training versions of the I-16, known as the UTI-4.

The I-16's main opponent in the summer sky of 1941 was the German Messerschmitt Bf 109, which had also undergone a series of upgrades since its birth in 1934. But the quality of the basic design allowed German engineers to create a much more formidable battle machine, which outclassed its Soviet opponent in service ceiling, rate of climb, and crucially, horizontal speed. This was largely due to better aerodynamics and a more powerful engine. For example the main versions of the I-16 had a maximum speed of 450–470km/h, while the Bf 109E had a maximum speed of 560–570km/h, and its upgrade, the Bf 109F, a maximum speed of 600km/h. Superiority in speed was the decisive factor in a dogfight, and it couldn't be compensated for by tactical tricks, so German pilots held the initiative: they could chase their opponents, attack swiftly from above and behind, and then gain altitude for a new attack – all without any fear of the enemy getting 'on their tail'. Meanwhile, pilots of 'Donkeys' could only passively defend each other by forming a defensive circle, or evade attacks via good horizontal manoeuvrability. It should also be noted that Messerschmitts, due to better aero-dynamics and greater weight, had a higher acceleration rate than the I-16 when diving, which meant German pilots always had a chance to disengage in unfavourable situations and escape.

In terms of armament, Messerschmitts had only a slight edge on the I-16. A Bf 109A-4 carried two wing-mounted 20mm MGFF cannon and two synchronized 7.92mm MG-17 machine guns, the weight of a one-second salvo being 2.37kg. But the Bf 109F-2, which replaced the 109A-4 (the 'Emile'), had a less formidable weight of fire at only 1.04kg. Meanwhile, the most common version of the I-16, the Type 24, was armed with two synchronized and two wing-mounted 7.62mm ShKAS machine guns, capable of delivering 1.43kg of shot each second. It should be noted, however, that Messerschmitts were more stable in flight than I-16s, making them a steadier weapons platform. Finally, the ammunition storage on a Messerschmitt exceeded that of the I-16: the former carrying 1,000 rounds for each MG plus 60 rounds for each cannon; the latter carrying only 450 rounds for each ShKAS.

Finally, when comparing the I-16 and Bf 109, it is important to mention another important aspect. By the outbreak of the Second World War all Messerschmitts were equipped with reliable two-way FuG-7 radios. This allowed German pilots to co-ordinate their activities during battle, and to receive guidance from ground observers. But the bulk of Soviet pilots did not have this luxury: out of almost 3,000 'Donkeys' in service with the Soviet Air Force, as few as 150 had RSI-3 Orel (Eagle) radios, as the Soviet factories failed to deliver them in larger numbers.

Another Polikarpov fighter of significant numbers in the pre-war Soviet Air Force was the I-153. This was a biplane dubbed 'Chajka' or 'Seagull', and the Western Military Districts had about 1,500 of them, accounting for 35 per cent of the total Soviet fighter force. Despite entering service as recently as 1938, the I-153's design was obsolete by some ten years, the only up-to-date element being its retractable landing gear.

Most 'Seagulls' had the same M-63 engines as the I-16 Type 24, but due to inferior aerodynamics the plane was slower: only 370km/h (435–440km/h at an altitude of 5,000m). This precluded the I-153 from successfully engaging German fighters or intercepting bombers. At the same time, the wing loading of the 'Seagull' was much lower than that of the 'Donkey', which meant better horizontal manoeuvrability. Thus an I-153 could complete a full circle in 13–14 seconds at 1,000m, while an I-16 took 16–18 seconds. But both had a rate of climb of approximately 14.7–15m/s.

A negative feature of the I-153 in comparison with monoplane fighters was impaired forward visibility caused by the upper wing. Although Polikarpov tried to fix the problem by giving the upper wing a prominent dip or bend in the middle (the so-called 'gull wing' that gave the plane its nickname), a significant part of the forward semi-sphere remained hidden from the pilot's view, hindering the spotting and observation of targets.

Needless to say, these inferior flight characteristics meant that 'Seagulls' stood little chance against Messerschmitts. And once engaged by the enemy, 'Seagulls' were unable to escape, making them easy prey. And so, useless in dogfights, the Air Force transferred all I-153s to ground assault regiments, where their armament (four machine guns of rifle calibre and two 25 or 50kg bombs) made them effective against soft targets. But by late 1941 the number of 'Seagulls' in front-line units dropped to 200, and a year later they had almost disappeared from Eastern Front skies.

A New Generation of Fighters

In 1939 several design bureaus began feverishly creating a new generation of fighters, based on battle experience gained in Spain and later at Khalkhin Gol. The result was a famous triad of aircraft: the I-200 (MiG-1), the I-26 (Yak-1), and the I-301 (LaGG-3). These fighters, as well as their direct descendants, were to bear the brunt of battle during the Great Patriotic War.

The size and general design of these three aircraft were similar (for example, all had water-cooled engines). A special feature was the use of timber and plywood in the airframe (in the late 1930s the USSR was the only country in the world using timber as the main material for fighter aircraft manufacture). On the one hand, this allowed for a simple cost-saving design; on the other, it made the airframe heavier. But the designers based their plans on the objective capabilities of Soviet aircraft factories, which had a sufficient amount of timber-processing equipment, but a high deficit of the kind of kit necessary for mass producing metallic parts. Lacking the capacity for producing large amounts of 'flying metal', the USSR planned for mass production of timber-framed planes: for few doubted that war was imminent.

Mikoyan-Gurevich I-200 or MiG-1

Originally conceived as a high altitude interceptor, the I-200 fighter – later known as the MiG-1 – was a descendant of the I-16, displaying certain 'family features'. For example, it inherited the 'Donkey's' fuselage, which was modified to accommodate a water-cooled engine.

According to a directive 'from above', Soviet designers were instructed to increase the amount of timber in their prototypes. Consequently the consoles of the I-200's wings were made from wood. Another negative feature of the I-200 was its heavy AM-35A engine, which at 830kg was almost 35 per cent heavier than the M-105P engine installed in the Yak-1 and LaGG-3. The I-200's top power – 1,200hp – was reached at an altitude of 5,000m, but for average altitudes (up to 4,000m) this was reduced to 1,100–1,150hp. The prototype managed to accelerate to a speed of 640km/h at an altitude of 7,800m, but the lower the altitude, the lower the plane's flight performance.

In an attempt to improve flight characteristics, the MiG-3 was introduced on the eve of Operation *Barbarossa*. One of the fighter's strengths was its high acceleration rate in a dive. A much heavier machine than a Messerschmitt, the MiG-3 was able to dive faster and then make a higher, sharper climb.

Despite some shortcomings, the MiG-3 was the most widespread 'new generation' Soviet fighter on the eve of the German invasion, some 1,363 machines being built during the first six months of 1941. And at dawn on 22 June 1941 some 917 MiG-3s were deployed in the five Western Military Districts.

Yakovlev I-26 or Yak-1

The first new generation fighter to go through tests was the I-26 (later renamed the Yak-1) designed by A.S. Yakovlev. Initially the I-26 was built to be fitted with the 1,250hp M-106 engine, but the engine builders failed to make the engine sufficiently reliable. Yakovlev ended up installing a weaker but more reliable M-105P, which had a power of 1,100hp at an altitude of 2,000m and 1,150hp at 4,000m.

The Yak-1 compared favourably with the I-16 with regard to flight performance, being stable and easily handled – ideal for novice pilots with little training. Before the war Yakovlev had specialized in flight training and sport aircraft, enabling him to produce a fighter that was both manoeuvrable and easy to control. In addition, take-off and landing were simpler and safer in a Yak-1 than in a 'Donkey' or MiG.

The Yak-1 model of 1941 was noticeably heavier than a Messerschmitt Bf 109 and its weaker engine meant that it lagged behind its principal opponent (though its speed was an improvement on the

I-16). The Yak-1 was also inferior to the Messerschmitt in rate of climb at all altitudes. And although it could complete a circle at the same speed as a Messerschmitt, the Yak-1's lack of automation made dogfights a complicated business demanding high levels of concentration (in comparison, a Messerschmitt Bf 109, with its automatic flaps, had a lower stall speed and was more stable in sharp turns and vertical aerobatic figures).

But the problems associated with early Yaks lay not just in flying characteristics. The first aircraft to enter service in 1941 were still very 'raw' and thus prone to technical problems, which were only gradually fixed as production progressed. These defects (for example, the ejection of oil from the gear valve) made life hard for both pilots and mechanics.

As for radios, the situation on Yak-1s was initially even worse than on the I-16, the first 1,000 machines having no radios at all. But installation of radio equipment became common by spring 1942 and obligatory by August 1942.

The Yak-1's armament, however, was on par with that of the Messerschmitt Bf 109F-4: one 20mm ShVAK engine-mounted cannon (120 rounds) and two synchronized ShKAS machine guns above the engine (750 rounds each). The weight of fire (1.99kg) was higher than that of the German fighter due to the higher rate of fire of Soviet weapons.

By the outbreak of the war the Soviet aircraft industry had produced 425 Yak-1 fighters, and on 22 June 1941 92 machines were fully operational in the Western Military Districts – but most were lost in the very first days of the war. Nevertheless, some 856 more Yaks were built in 1941. Indeed, the descendant of the Yak-1, the Yak-9, became the most mass-produced Soviet fighter of all time, some 16,769 machines being in total (14,579 during the war).

Lavochkin-Gorbunov-Gudkov I-301 or LaGG-3

The most outstanding representative of wartime 'timber style' in Soviet fighter aircraft was the I-301, designed by S.A. Lavochkin, V.P. Gorbunov and M.I. Gudkov. It was designated LaGG-3 in serial production and later versions included the La-5 and La-7. The LaGG-3's airframe was almost completely made of timber, with crucial parts processed with Bakelite lacquer. This novel wood laminate construction was more durable than regular timber, incombustible, and didn't rot. It was, however, much heavier and pilots joked that LaGG (an acronym of the designers' names – Lavochkin-Gorbunov-Gudkov) stood for 'Lakirovanny garantirovanny grob' – 'Guaranteed lacquered coffin'!

The full wooden wing of the LaGG-3 (with plywood surfaces) was analogous to that of the Yak-1 (the only difference being that the LaGG's wings were constructed in two sections), while the fuselage was the same as the MiG-3's.

But the LaGG's armament was formidable, consisting of a large-calibre BK machine gun, which was installed between the 'V' of the cylinders, and two synchronized ShKAS machine guns. Consequently the weight of fire was 2.65kg, making the LaGG superior to all serial Soviet fighters, as well as the 1941 version of the Messerschmitt Bf 109.

Just like Yakovlev, Lavochkin, Gorbunov and Gudkov were obliged to install the relatively weak M-105P engine, having originally designed their prototype for the strong M-106 engine, which subsequently proved unusable due to unreliability. But this enforced change of specification harmed the LaGG's performance more than it did the Yak-1. In short, the LaGG-3 was too heavy for its engine. As a result the fighter was slow, somewhat inert and hard to control, reacting sluggishly to movements of the joystick. In particular, the plane was difficult to pull out of a dive, and if the stick was pulled too hard, tended to fall into a spin. As a consequence sharp turns were difficult to perform on the LaGG.

Thus, when the LaGG-3 was first committed to combat in July 1941, it was completely outclassed by the Messerschmitt Bf 109 (and was inferior to Yak fighters in all but firepower). Its rate of climb at ground level was as low as 8.5m/s, while top speed was 474km/h. The celebrated fighter ace D.A. Kudymov – who began the war on LaGGs – expressed a common view when he declared: 'We envied those pilots among us who were lucky to fly Yak-1s; pilots in those aircraft confidently engaged German aircraft of any model, despite numerical superiority of the enemy.'

Kudymov probably over-dramatized the situation in his last sentence, but the weighty LaGG-3 fighter was dubbed an 'Iron' by angry pilots.

In fact, the whole history of the plane's further development was a constant struggle to decrease its weight. As a consequence the LaGG lost both firepower and fuel, effectively decreasing its tactical assets.

By April 1942 it had become obvious that the fighter could not be improved in its existing shape, so an order was issued terminating production in favour of the Yak-7. But the LaGG was rescued by a radical change of engine: the 14 cylinder radial air-cooled M-82. By now Gorbunov and Gudkov were off the project, so the upgraded fighter was launched as the La-5. Now the reborn Soviet fighter could compete with Messerschmitts in horizontal manoeuvrability, and all machines were equipped with radios.

But the La-5 had serious drawbacks. Perhaps the most serious being bad thermal isolation of the engine, lack of air ventilation in the cockpit, and a canopy that was impossible to open at speeds over 350km/h. To make matters worse, exhaust gas often entered the cockpit due to poor insulation of the engine compartment. Consequently pilots ignored orders and frequently flew with their canopies open ...

Featured Aircraft – Quick Reference Guide

Designer	Model	AKA	Type	Country
Dornier	Do 215		Updated version of the Do 17 twin-engined light bomber	Germany
Dornier	Do 217		Twin-engined heavy bomber	Germany
Douglas			Military transport	USA
Fiesler	Fi 156	'Storch' ('Stork')	Short-range reconnaissance	Germany
Focke-Wulf	FW 190	'Fokker' (Misnomer applied to the plane by Russian pilots)	Single-seat fighter	Germany
Heinkel	He 111		Twin-engined bomber	Germany
Hawker	Hurricane		Single-seat fighter	Great Britain
Polikarpov	I-5		Biplane fighter	USSR
Polikarpov	I-15		Biplane fighter	USSR
Polikarpov	I-16	'Ishak' ('Donkey')	Single-seat fighter	USSR
Yakovlev	I-26	Yak-1	Prototype of the Yak-1 single-seat fighter	USSR
Polikarpov	I-153	'Chajka' ('Seagull')	Biplane fighter	USSR

Designer	Model	AKA	Type	Country
Mikoyan-Gurevich	I-200	MiG-1	Single-seat fighter	USSR
Lavochkin-Gorbunov-Gudkov	I-301	LaGG-3	Prototype of the LaGG-3 single-seat fighter	USSR
Ilyushin	Il-2	'Shturmovik'	Two-seat assault bomber	USSR
Junkers	Ju 87	'Stuka'	Two-seat dive bomber	Germany
Junkers	Ju 88		Twin-engined bomber	Germany
Lavochkin	La-5		Updated version of the LaGG-3 single-seat fighter	USSR
Lavochkin	La-7		Updated version of the La-5 single-seat fighter	USSR
Lavochkin	La-9		Updated version of the La-7 single-seat fighter	USSR
Lavochkin-Gorbunov-Gudkov	LaGG-3	I-301	Single-seat fighter	USSR
Lisunov	Li-2		Russian version of the Douglas DC-3 transport, made under license	USSR
Messerschmitt	Bf 109E	'Emil'	Single-seat fighter	Germany
Messerschmitt	Bf 109F	'Friedrich'	Updated version of the 109E	Germany
Messerschmitt	Bf 109G	'Gustav'	Updated version of the 109F	Germany
Messerschmitt	Me 110		Twin-engined bomber	Germany
Mikoyan-Gurevich	MiG-1	I-200	Single-seat fighter	USSR
Mikoyan-Gurevich	MiG-2		Updated version of the MiG-1	USSR
Mikoyan-Gurevich	MiG-3		Updated version of the MiG-2	USSR
Bell	P-39	'Airacobra' (USAAF) 'Aircobra' (RAF) 'Cobra' (Colloquial)	Single-seat fighter	USA

Designer	Model	AKA	Type	Country
Bell	P-39Q		Updated version of the P-39. Further modifications created a 'Q' sub-series	USA
Curtiss	P-40	'Warhawk' (USAAF) 'Tomahawk' (RAF) 'Kittyhawk' (RAF)	Single-seat fighter in production between 1939–44. Known as the 'Warhawk' in the US, the British version was dubbed the 'Tomahawk' and its upgrade the 'Kittyhawk'	USA
Petlyakov	Pe-2	'Peshka' ('Pawn')	Twin-engined long-range dive bomber	USSR
Polikarpov	Po-2	U-2 'Kukuruznik' ('Maize Cutter')	General purpose two-seat biplane. Originally known as the U-2, it was renamed the Po-2 in 1944. The Germans referred to the plane as the 'Nähmaschine' ('Sewing Machine') on account of its rattling sound	USSR
Polikarpov	R-5		Biplane used primarily for reconnaissance	USSR
Tupolev	SB	ANT-40	Twin-engined three-seat bomber. 'SB' stands for 'Skorostnoi Bombardirovschik' or 'high speed bomber'	USSR
Tupolev	TB-3	ANT-6	Twin-engined four-seat heavy bomber	USSR
Polikarpov	U-2		Original designation of the Po-2 biplane	USSR
Yakovlev	UT-2		Standard Soviet trainer	USSR
Polikarpov	UTI-4		Two-seat trainer converted from the I-16	USSR
Yakovlev	Yak-1	I-26	Single-seat fighter	USSR
Yakovlev	Yak-3		Updated version of the Yak-1	USSR

Designer	Model	AKA	Type	Country
Yakovlev	Yak-7	UTI-26	Initially a two-seat training version of the Yak-1 (also used for combat and reconnaissance), a single-seat fighter was later produced	USSR
Yakovlev	Yak-9		Updated version of the single-seat Yak-7 fighter	USSR

Glossary

Alexander Nevski, Order of:	Established in July 1942 and awarded to commanders (from platoon to division level) for skilful handling of troops in action.
Budyonovka:	Cloth helmet with pointed top, favoured by Bolshevik troops in the Russian Civil War.
Chajka:	Russian word meaning 'Seagull' – a colloquial term for the Polikarpov I-153 fighter (see below).
'Chicken':	Colloquial term for a pilot's insignia, consisting of a badge depicting a propeller, wings and crossed sabres in gold, on a blue background, surmounted by a red star and worn on the left sleeve.
Dacha:	Private holiday home or villa.
'Donkey':	Colloquial term for the I-16 fighter.
'Emil':	Nickname of the Messerschmitt Bf 109E fighter.
'Fokker':	Colloquial name for the FW 190 as used by Russian pilots. But the term is a misnomer as there is no connection between the Dutch aircraft designer Anthony Fokker (1890–1939) and the Focke-Wulf FW 190.
'Friedrich':	Nickname of the Messerschmitt Bf 109F fighter.
Front:	Soviet army group.
Frontovik:	Colloquial term for a front-line soldier.

Gold Star/Hero of
  the Soviet Union: Established in April 1934 as an honorary title, the Gold Star medal was instituted in August 1939. Awarded to civilians and military personnel for personal or collective deeds of heroism in the cause of Socialism. Privileges included a pension, priority on the housing list, reduced taxes, free bus transportation and a free annual trip to a sanitarium.

Great Patriotic War,
  Order of the: Established in May 1942 with 1st and 2nd Class distinctions. Awarded to officers and men of the Armed Forces, the former grade for skilful command, the latter for personal valour.

'Gustav': Nickname of the Messerschmitt Bf 109G fighter.

House of Culture: Institutionalized focal point for state-sponsored cultural events.

Ishak: Russian word meaning 'Donkey' – a colloquial term for the I-16 fighter ('Ishachok' meaning 'Little Donkey').

Kolkhoz: Collectively-owned farm.

Kombat: Battalion commander in the Red Army.

Komsomol: Young Communist League.

Kulaks: Land-owning farmers persecuted by the Soviet state.

Lenin, Order of: Established in April 1930 as the highest decoration of the Soviet Union. Awarded to civilians and military personnel for outstanding services to the state.

Messer: Colloquial Russian term for the Messerschmitt Bf 109 fighter.

Moskal: Ukrainian slang for a Russian (pejorative).

Nagant: Belgian hand-gun widely used in Russia, the shortened form, 'Nagan', being synonymous with 'revolver'.

NKVD: Acronym for *Narodny Kommissariat Vnutrennykh Del* – 'People's Commissariat of Internal Affairs' – the Soviet secret police from 1934 to 1943.

Oberfeldwebel:	German NCO rank equivalent to sergeant-major in the British Army.
Osoaviakhim:	The 'Society for Assistance to the Army, Aviation and Fleet'.
Osobnyak:	NKVD representative attached to military units with powers of arrest and prosecution.
Peshka:	Colloquial term for the Petlyakov Pe-2 bomber, meaning 'Pawn'.
Politruk:	Political commissar.
Polizei:	German-organized police force of collaborationists.
Red Banner, Order of the:	Established in August 1924 as the first order of the new Soviet state. Awarded to military personnel for courage and self-sacrifice in combat.
Red Star, Order of the:	Established in April 1930 and awarded to military personnel for conspicuous service in defence of the state.
'Seagull':	Colloquial term for the Polikarpov I-153 fighter.
Shtrafbat:	Acronym for *shtrafnoi batalyon* – a punishment battalion.
Shtrafniks:	Soldiers of a *Shtrafbat* punishment battalion.
Shturmovik:	Colloquial term for ground assault aircraft, in particular the Ilyushin Il-2.
SMERSh:	Soviet counter-intelligence unit formed in April 1943.
Sovkhoz:	State-owned farm.
Stavka:	Central Soviet Military Command.
Stuka:	The German Ju 87 dive bomber.
Suvorov, Order of:	Established in July 1942 and awarded to Army commanders for outstanding merit in directing combat operations.
Wehrmacht:	The German Armed Forces as a whole.

Index